43

Moorcock's Books of Martyrs is a new collection, made by Michael Moorcock himself, of some of his own favourite stories. They range far and wide across eras and universes, and if there is a linking theme it is one of martyrdom. (How else could he link stories about Jesus Christ, Alexander the Great and Jimi Hendrix?) From space opera to spaced-out rock and roll, from A.D. 29 to Doomsday, from the claustrophobic contents of a madman's brain to the agoraphobic infinity of the universe, Moorcock finds ideas which could have occurred to nobody else but which will be enjoyed by everyone.

ALSO BY MICHAEL MOORCOCK IN QUARTET EDITIONS

The Sleeping Sorceress
The War Lord of the Air
The Land Leviathan
The Bull and the Spear
The Oak and the Ram
The Sword and the Stallion
The English Assassin
A Cure for Cancer
The Lives and Times of Jerry Cornelius
The Sailor on the Seas of Fate

MOORCOCK'S BOOK OF MARTYRS

MICHAEL MOORCOCK

QUARTET BOOKS LONDON

First published by Quartet Books Limited 1976
27 Goodge Street, London W1P 1FD

ISBN 0 704 31265 4

'A Dead Singer' first appeared in *Factions*, 1974; 'The Greater Conqueror' in *Science Fantasy*, 1962; 'Behold the Man' in *New Worlds*, 1966; 'Good-bye, Miranda' in *New Worlds*, 1964; 'Flux' and 'Islands' in *New World*, 1963; and 'Waiting for the End of Time . . .' in *Visions of Tomorrow*, 1970.

This book is dedicated
to the memories of
John the Bog,
Smiling Mike
and
Mongezi Feza

Printed in Great Britain by
Richard Clay (The Chaucer Press) Ltd,
Bungay, Suffolk

CONTENTS

INTRODUCTION

It could be argued that one of the main themes of nineteenth-century fiction had to do with the attempt of the individual to find personal freedom in what we should today call a repressive society, whereas in the Western democracies the problem of many contemporary people, the heirs to the great radical and libertarian movements of the early years of this century, is how we should use our freedom. Like writers who will invent alternative repressions in order to continue writing in a traditional mode, some will give up that freedom rather than face the problem – identifying with any sort of orthodoxy, whether political, religious, or quasi-religious, to demand a denial of their individuality. Ironically others will lose their freedom by allowing themselves to be used as totem figures by those who see them as personifications of the free spirit they themselves yearn to be: the fate of many artists who become public figures only to be, in different ways, destroyed by the very public which worships them. Self-consciousness, which makes actors of us all, turns the innocent Fool into the self-destructive Demon.

The greater the public attention one receives, the harder it is to retain a clear image of one's own identity. Although Glogaeur in 'Behold the Man' has a deep-seated need to have the truth of the gospels affirmed, he is manipulated, right from the moment that he meets John the Baptist, into becoming the messiah the people need.

My Cornelius stories are, among other things, about the search of the free spirit for an individual morality not at odds with the demands of society, for to make a virtue of alienation (in the Byronic manner) is to lose perspective quite as easily as if one makes a virtue of orthodoxy (in the Kipling manner). Orthodoxy, of course, forces the individual into the Byronic pose; aggressive men can make 'hard' women; hysterical authorities can turn peaceful demonstrations into riots. Repressive authority creates violence. Chaos against Law – a balance must be struck between the two. My stories are generally about people who seek that balance. From Elric, through my few actual sf novels, through the entire Eternal Champion cycle, to Jerry Cornelius, the heroes and heroines – Fools all – try to find equilibrium between what they believe and what the world wishes them to accept, and those who fail (in my earlier work at least) often die as a result of their failure. The Cornelius family survives to seek again because, like me, it is essentially optimistic. I believe that eventually we shall all find a way to be ourselves while serving the needs of our society: A time will come when the orthodox shall learn to tolerate the unorthodox and *vice versa* in what is no more, I suppose, than an ideal liberal democracy.

Some of the 'martyrs' of these stories are primarily people who seek to impose a private vision on the world and who suffer accordingly. Some of them (there is at least one obvious example) end up creating an orthodoxy quite as extreme as anything they have attempted to overthrow. Both Karl Glogaeur and Max File attempt to create a new reality. Both succeed (though in the case of 'Flux' – rewritten at the request of a magazine editor when I was young – the theme is somewhat simplified) and both pay a price for that success. Another simpler theme to be found in several of these stories is that of the individual without much natural aggression who is crushed by an intolerant world. The only full-fledged fantasy story here, 'The Greater Conqueror' makes use almost wholly of metaphor and symbolism to carry its theme – it is in the nature of the form – but none the less Alexander can be seen as an individual manipulated and destroyed by the demands of a powerful public will.

Inevitably confused between self and society, self and environment, the modern individual finds it increasingly difficult to discover a satisfactory borderline between the demands of society and the demands of instinct. There are no easily isolated evils. So far as their specific conclusions are concerned the great eighteenth- and nineteenth-century radicals have been proved at very least unsophisticated. Too many visionary idealists have died in this century because their private visions have been judged incompatible with the terrifying orthodoxies they have helped establish. Too many people seem unable to make any other response to the suffering and brutality of the world than that of violent political action or a falling back on such maxims as 'To thine own self be true'. My response, of course, is to write books and, in the act of writing, to hope to discover at least a few clues which will help solve the dilemma; to encourage a little more tolerance between those who are of an orthodox disposition and those who are not, for society, it seems to me, can make good use of both temperaments. The world probably has need of saints and sinners – but I look forward to the day when it will no longer need martyrs of any persuasion.

MICHAEL MOORCOCK
Ladbroke Grove
January 1976

A DEAD SINGER

In memory, among others, of Smiling Mike and John the Bog

CHAPTER ONE

'It's not the speed, Jimi,' said Shakey Mo, 'it's the H you got to look out for.'

Jimi was amused. 'Well, it never did me much good.'

'It didn't do you no harm in the long run.' Shakey Mo laughed. He could hardly hold on to the steering wheel.

The big Mercedes camper took another badly lit bend. It was raining hard against the windscreen. He switched on the lamps. With his left hand he fumbled a cartridge from the case on the floor beside him and slotted it into the stereo. The heavy, driving drumming and moody synthesizers of Hawkwind's latest album, made Mo feel much better. 'That's the stuff for energy,' said Mo.

Jimi leaned back. Relaxed, he nodded. The music filled the camper.

Shakey Mo kept getting speed hallucinations on the road ahead. Armies marched across his path; Nazis set up road blocks; scampering children chased balls; big fires suddenly started and ghouls appeared and disappeared. He had a bad time controlling himself enough to keep on driving through it all. The images were familiar and he wasn't freaked out by them. He was content to be driving for Jimi. Since his comeback (or resurrection as Mo privately called it) Jimi hadn't touched a guitar or sung a note, preferring to listen to the other people's music. He was taking a long while to recover from what had happened to him in Ladbroke Grove. Only recently his colour had started to return and he was still wearing the white silk shirt and jeans in which he'd been dressed when Shakey Mo first saw him, standing casually on the cowling of the Imperial Airways flying boat as it taxied towards the landing stage on Derwentwater. What a summer that had been, thought Mo. Beautiful.

The tape began to go round for the second time. Mo touched the stud to switch tracks, then thought better of it. He turned the stereo off altogether.

'Nice one.' Jimi was looking thoughtful again. He was almost asleep as he lay stretched out over the bench seat, his hooded eyes fixed on the black road.

'It's got to build up again soon,' said Mo. 'It can't last, can it? I mean, everything's so dead. Where's the energy going to come from, Jimi?'

'It's where it keeps going to that bothers me, man. You know?'

'I guess you're right.' Mo didn't understand.

But Jimi had to be right.

Jimi had known what he was doing, even when he died. Eric Burden had gone on TV to say so. 'Jimi knew it was time to go,' he'd said. It was like that with the records and performances. Some of them hadn't seemed to be as tight as others; some of them were even a bit rambling. Hard to turn on to. But Jimi had known what he was doing. You had to have faith in him.

Mo felt the weight of his responsibilities. He was a good roadie, but there were better roadies than him. More together people who could be trusted with a big secret. Jimi hadn't spelt it out but it was obvious he felt that the world wasn't yet ready for his return. But why hadn't Jimi chosen one of the really ace roadies? Everything had to be prepared for the big gig. Maybe at Shea Stadium or the Albert Hall or the Paris Olympia? Anyway, some classic venue. Or at a festival? A special festival celebrating the resurrection. Woodstock or Glastonbury. Probably something new altogether, some new holy place. India, maybe? Jimi would say when the time came. After Jimi had contacted him and told him where to be picked up, Mo had soon stopped asking questions. With all his old gentleness, Jimi had turned the questions aside. He had been kind, but it was clear he hadn't wanted to answer.

Mo respected that.

The only really painful request Jimi had made was that Mo stop playing his old records, including *Hey, Joe!* the first single. Previously there hadn't been a day when Mo hadn't put something of Jimi's on. In his room in Lancaster Road, in the truck when he was roading for Light and later The Deep Fix, even when he'd gone to the House during his short-lived conversion to Scientology he'd been able to plug his earbead into his cassette recorder for an hour or so. While Jimi's physical presence made up for a lot and stopped the worst of the withdrawal symptoms, it was still difficult. No amount of mandrax, speed or booze could counter his need for the music and, consequently, the shakes were getting just a little bit worse each day. Mo sometimes felt that he was paying some kind of price for Jimi's trust in him. That was good karma so he didn't mind. He was used to the shakes anyway. You could get used to anything. He looked at his sinewy, tattooed arms stretched before him, the hands gripping the steering wheel. The world snake was wriggling again. Black, red, and green, it coiled slowly down his skin, round his wrist and began to inch towards his elbow. He fixed his eyes back on the road.

CHAPTER TWO

Jimi had fallen into a deep sleep. He lay along the seat behind Mo, his head resting on the empty guitar case. He was breathing heavily, almost as if something were pressing down on his chest.

The sky ahead was wide and pink. In the distance was a line of blue hills. Mo was tired. He could feel the old paranoia creeping in. He took a fresh joint from the ledge and lit it, but he knew that dope wouldn't do a lot of good. He needed a couple of hours sleep himself.

Without waking Jimi, Mo pulled the truck into the side of the road, near a wide, shallow river full of flat, white limestone rocks. He opened his door and climbed slowly to the grass. He wasn't sure where they were; maybe somewhere in Yorkshire. There were hills all around. It was a mild autumn morning but Mo felt cold. He clambered down to the bank and knelt there, cupping his hands in the clear water, sucking up the river. He stretched out and put his tattered straw hat over his face. It was a very heavy scene at the moment. Maybe that was why it was taking Jimi so long to get it together.

Mo felt much better when he woke up. It must have been noon. The sun was hot on his skin. He took a deep breath of the rich air and cautiously removed his hat from his face. The black Mercedes camper with its chrome trimming was still on the grass near the road. Mo's mouth felt dry. He had another drink of water and rose, shaking the silver drops from his brown fingers. He trudged slowly to the truck, pulled back the door and looked over the edge of the driver's seat. Jimi wasn't there, but sounds came behind the partition. Mo climbed across the two seats and slid open the connecting door. Jimi sat on one of the beds. He had erected the table and was drawing in a big red notebook. His smile was remote as Mo entered.

'Sleep good?' he asked.

Mo nodded. 'I needed it.'

'Sure,' said Jimi. 'Maybe I ought to do a little driving.'

'It's okay. Unless you want to make better time.'

'No.'

'I'll get some breakfast,' said Mo. 'Are you hungry?'

Jimi shook his head. All through the summer, since he had left the flying boat and got into the truck beside Mo, Jimi appeared to have eaten nothing. Mo cooked himself some sausages and beans on the little Calor stove, opening the back door so that the smell wouldn't fill the camper. 'I might go for a swim,' he said as he brought his plate to the table and sat as far away from Jimi as possible, so as not to disturb him.

'Okay,' said Jimi, absorbed in his drawing.

'What you doing? Looks like a comic strip. I'm really into comics.'

Jimi shrugged. 'Just doodling, man. You know.'

Mo finished his food. 'I'll get some comics next time we stop on the motorway. Some of the new ones are really far out, you know.'

'Yeah?' Jimi's smile was sardonic.

'Really far out. Cosmic wars, time warps. All the usual stuff but different, you know. Better. Bigger. More spectacular. Sensational, man. Oh, you want to see them. I'll get some.'

'Too much,' said Jimi distantly but it was obvious he hadn't been listening. He closed the note-book and sat back against the vinyl cushions, folding his arms across his white silk chest. As if it occurred to him that he might have hurt Mo's feelings, he added: 'Yeah, I used to be into comics a lot. You seen the Jap kind? Big fat books. Oh, man – they are *really* far out. Kids burning. Rape. All that stuff.' He laughed shaking his head. 'Oh, man!'

'Yeah?' Mo laughed hesitantly.

'Right!' Jimi went to the door, placing a hand either side of the frame and looking into the day. 'Where are we, Mo? It's a little like Pennsylvania. The Delaware Valley. Ever been there?'

'Never been to the States.'

'Is that right?'

'Somewhere in Yorkshire, I think. Probably north of Leeds. That could be the Lake District over there.'

'Is that where I came through?'

'Derwentwater.'

'Well, well.' Jimi chuckled.

Jimi was livelier today. Maybe it was taking him time to store up all the energy he'd need when he finally decided to reveal himself to the world. Their driving had been completely at random. Jimi had let Mo decide where to go. They had been all over Wales, the Peaks, The West Country, most parts of the Home Counties, everywhere except London. Jimi had been reluctant to go to London. It was obvious why. Bad memories. Mo had been into town a few times, leaving the Mercedes and Jimi in a suburban layby and walking and hitching into London to get his mandies and his speed. When he could he scored some coke. He liked to get behind a snort or two once in a while. In Finch's on the corner of Portobello Road he'd wanted to tell his old mates about Jimi, but Jimi had said to keep quiet about it, so when people had asked him what he was doing, where he was living these days, he'd had to give vague answers. There was no problem about money. Jimi didn't have any but Mo had got a lot selling the white Dodge convertible. The Deep Fix had given it to him after they'd stopped going on the road. And there was a big bag of dope in the truck, too. Enough to last two people for months, though Jimi didn't seem to have any taste for that, either.

Jimi came back into the gloom of the truck. 'What d'you say we get on the road again?'

Mo took his plate, knife and fork down to the river, washed them and stashed them back in the locker. He got into the driver's seat and turned the key. The Wankel engine started at once. The Mercedes pulled smoothly away, still heading north, bumping off the grass and back on to the asphalt. They were on a narrow road suitable only for one way traffic, but there was nobody behind them and nobody ahead of them until they left this road and turned on to the A65, making for Kendal.

'You don't mind the Lake District?' Mo asked.

'Suits me,' said Jimi. 'I'm the mad Gull Warrior, man.' He smiled. 'Maybe we should make for the ocean?'

'It's not far from here.' Mo pointed west. 'Morecambe Bay?'

CHAPTER THREE

The cliff tops were covered in turf as smooth as a fairway. Below them the sea sighed. Jimi and Mo were in good spirits, looning around like kids.

In the distance, round the curve of the bay, were the towers and fun-fairs and penny arcades of Morecambe, but here it was deserted and still, apart from the occasional cry of a gull.

Mo laughed, then cried out nervously as Jimi danced so near to the cliff edge it seemed he'd fall over.

'Take it easy, Jimi.'

'Shit, man. They can't kill me.'

He had a broad, euphoric smile on his face and he looked really healthy. 'They can't kill Jimi, man!'

Mo remembered him on stage. In total command. Moving through the strobes, his big guitar stuck out in front of him, pointing at each individual member of the audience, making each kid feel that he was in personal touch with Jimi.

'Right!' Mo began to giggle.

Jimi hovered on the edge, still flapping his outstretched arms. 'I'm the boy they boogie to. Oh, man! There ain't nothing they can do to me!'

'Right!'

Jimi came zooming round and flung himself down on the turf next to Mo. He was panting. He was grinning. It's coming back, Mo. All fresh and new.'

Mo nodded, still giggling.

'I just know it's there, man.'

Mo looked up. The gulls were everywhere. They were screaming. They took on the aspect of an audience. He hated them. They were so thick in the sky now.

'Don't let them fucking feathers stick in your throat,' said Mo, suddenly sullen. He got up and returned to the truck.

'Mo. What's the matter with you, man?'

Jimi was concerned as ever, but that only brought Mo down more. It was Jimi's kindness which had killed him the first time. He'd been polite to everyone. He couldn't help it. Really hung-up people had got off on him. And they'd drained Jimi dry.

'They'll get you again, man,' said Mo. 'I know they will. Every time. There isn't a thing you can do about it. No matter how much energy you build up, you know, they'll still suck it out of you and moan for more. They want your blood, man. They want your sperm and your bones and your flesh, man. They'll take you, man. They'll eat you up again.'

'No. I'll – no, not this time.'

'Sure.' Mo sneered.

'Man, are you trying to bring me down.'

Mo began to twitch. 'No. But . . .'

'Don't worry, man, okay?' Jimi's voice was soft and assured.

'I can't put it into words, Jimi. It's this, sort of, premonition, you know.'

'What good did words ever do for anybody?' Jimi laughed his old, deep laugh. 'You *are* crazy, Mo. Come on, let's get back in the truck. Where do you want to head for?'

But Mo couldn't reply. He sat at the steering wheel and stared through the windscreen at the sea and the gulls.

Jimi was conciliatory. 'Look, Mo, I'll be cool about it, right? I'll take it easy, or maybe you think I don't need you?'

Mo didn't know why he was so down all of a sudden.

'Mo, you stay with me, wherever I go,' said Jimi.

CHAPTER FOUR

Outside Carlisle they saw a hitchhiker, a young guy who looked really wasted. He was leaning on a signpost. He had enough energy to raise his hand. Mo thought they should stop for him. Jimi said: 'If you want to,' and went into the back of the truck, closing the door as Mo pulled in for the hitchhiker.

Mo said: 'Where you going?'

The hitchhiker said: 'What about Fort William, man?'

Mo said: 'Get in.'

The hitchhiker said his name was Chris. 'You with a band, man?' He glanced round the cabin at the old stickers and the stereo, at Mo's tattoos, his faded face-paint, his Cawthorn T-shirt, his beaded jacket, his worn jeans with washed-out patches on them, the leather cowboy boots which Mo had bought at the Emperor of Wyoming in Notting Hill Gate last year.

'Used to road for The Deep Fix,' said Mo.

The hitchhiker's eyes were sunken and the sockets were red. His thick black hair was long and hung down to his pale face. He wore a torn Wrangler denim shirt, a dirty white Levi jacket and both legs of his jeans had holes in the knees. He had moccasins on his feet. He was nervous and eager.

'Yeah?'

'Right,' said Mo.

'What's in the back?' Chris turned to look at the door. 'Gear?'

'You could say that.'

'I've been hitching for three days, night and day,' said Chris. He had an oil- and weather-stained khaki pack on his lap.

'D'you mind if I get some kip some time?'

'No,' said Mo. There was a service station ahead. He decided to pull in and fill the Merc up. By the time he got to the pumps Chris was asleep.

As he waited to get back into the traffic, Mo crammed his mouth full of pills. Some of them fell from his hand on to the floor. He didn't bother to pick them up. He was feeling bleak.

Chris woke when they were going through Glasgow.

'Is this Glasgow?'

Mo nodded. He couldn't keep the paranoia down. He glared at the cars ahead as they moved slowly through the streets. Every window of every shop had a big steel mesh grill on it. The pubs were like bunkers. He was really pissed off without knowing why.

'Where you going yourself?' Chris asked.

'Fort William?'

'Lucky for me. Know where I can score any grass in Fort William?'

Mo reached forward and pushed a tobacco tin along the edge towards the hitchhiker. 'You can have that.'

Chris took the tin and opened it. 'Far out! You mean it? And the skins?'

'Sure,' said Mo. He hated Chris, he hated everybody. He knew the mood would pass.

'Oh, wow! Thanks, man.' Chris put the tin in his pack.

'I'll roll one when we're out of the city, okay?'

'Okay.'

'Who are you working for now?' said Chris. 'A band?'

'No.'

'You on holiday?'

The kid was too speedy. Probably it was just his lack of sleep. 'Sort of,' he said.

'Me, too. Well, it started like that. I'm at university. Exeter. Or was. I decided to drop out. I'm not going back to that shit heap. One term was enough for me. I thought of heading for the Hebrides. Someone I know's living in a commune out there, on one of the islands. They got their own sheep, goats, a cow. Nobody getting off on them. You know. Really free. It seems okay to me.'

Mo nodded.

Chris pushed back his black, greasy hair. 'I mean compare something like that with a place like this. How do people stand it, man. Fucking hell.'

Mo didn't answer. He moved forward, changing gear as the lights changed.

'Amazing,' said Chris. He saw the case of cartridges at his feet. 'Can I play some music?'

'Go ahead,' said Mo.'

Chris picked out an old album, *Who's Next*. He tried to slide it into the slot the wrong way round. Mo took it from his hand and put it in the right way. He felt better when the music started. He noticed, out of the corner of his eye, that Chris tried to talk for a while before he realized he couldn't be heard.

Mo let the tape play over and over again as they drove away from Glasgow. Chris rolled joints and Mo smoked a little, beginning to get on top of his paranoia. By about four in the afternoon, he was feeling better and he switched off the stereo. They were driving beside Loch Lomond. The bracken was turning brown and shone like brass where the sun touched it. Chris had fallen asleep again, but he woke up as the music stopped. 'Far out.' He dug the scenery. 'Fucking far out.' He wound his window down. 'This is the first time I've been to Scotland.'

'Yeah?' said Mo.

'How long before we reach Fort William, man?'

'A few hours. Why are you heading for Fort William?'

'I met this chick. She comes from there. Her old man's a chemist or something.'

Mo said softly, on impulse: 'Guess who I've got in the back.'

'A chick?'

'No.'

'Who?'

'Jimi Hendrix.'

Chris's jaw dropped. He looked at Mo and snorted, willing to join in the joke. 'No? Really? Hendrix, eh? What is it, a refrigerated truck?' He was excited by the fantasy. 'You think if we thaw him out he'll play something for us?' He shook his head, grinning.

'He is sitting in the back there. Alive. I'm roading for him.'

'Really?'

'Yeah.'

'Fantastic.' Chris was half convinced. Mo laughed. Chris looked at the door. After that, he was silent for a while.

Something like a half an hour later, he said: 'Hendrix was the best, you know. He was the king, man. Not just the music, but the style, too. Everything. I couldn't believe it when I heard he died. I still can't believe it, you know.'

'Sure,' said Mo. 'Well, he's back.'

'Yeah?' Again Chris laughed uncertainly. 'In there? Can I see him?'

'He's not ready, yet.'

'Sure,' said Chris.

It was dark when they reached Fort William. Chris staggered down from the truck. 'Thanks, man. That's really nice, you know. Where are you staying?'

'I'm moving on,' said Mo. 'See you.'

'Yeah. See you.' Chris still had that baffled look on his face.

Mo smiled to himself as he started the camper, heading for Oban. Once they were moving the door opened and Jimi clambered over the seats to sit beside him.

'You told that kid about me?'

'He didn't believe me,' said Mo.

Jimi shrugged.

It began to rain again.

CHAPTER FIVE

They lay together in the damp heather looking out over the hills. There was nobody for miles; no roads, towns or houses. The air was still and empty save for a hawk drifting so high above them it was almost out of sight.

'This'll do, eh?' said Mo. 'It's fantastic.'

Jimi smiled gently. 'It's nice,' he said.

Mo took a Mars Bar from his pocket and offered it to Jimi who shook his head. Mo began to eat the Mars Bar.

'What d'you think I am, man?' said Jimi.

'How d'you mean?'

'Devil or angel? You know.'

'You're Jimi,' said Mo. 'That's good enough for me, man.'

'Or just a ghost,' said Jimi. 'Maybe I'm just a ghost.'

Mo began to shake. 'No,' he said.

'Or a killer?' Jimi got up and struck a pose. 'The Sonic Assassin. Or the messiah, maybe.' He laughed. 'You wanna hear my words of wisdom?'

'That's not what it's about,' said Mo, frowning. 'Words. You just have to be there, Jimi. On the stage. With your guitar. You're above all that stuff – all the hype. Whatever you do – it's right, you know.'

'If you say so, Mo.' Jimi was on some kind of downer. He lowered himself to the heather and sat there cross-legged, smoothing his white jeans, picking mud off his black patent-leather boots. 'What is all this *Easy Rider* crap anyway? What are we doing here?'

'You didn't like *Easy Rider*?' Mo was astonished.

'The best thing since *Lassie Come Home*.' Jimi shrugged. 'All it ever proved was that Hollywood could still turn 'em out, you know. They got a couple of fake freaks and made themselves a lot of money. A rip off, man. And the kids fell for it. What does that make me?'

'You never ripped anybody off, Jimi.'

'Yeah? How d'you know?'

'Well, you never did.'

'All that low energy shit creeping in everywhere. Things are bad.' Jimi had changed the subject, making a jump Mo couldn't follow. 'People all over the Grove playing nothing but fake fifties crap, Simon and Garfunkel. Jesus Christ! Was it ever worth doing?'

'Things go in waves. You can't be up the whole time.'

'Sure,' Jimi sneered. 'This one's for all the soldiers fighting in Chicago. And Milwaukee. And New York ... And Vietnam. Down with War and Pollution. What was all that about?'

'Well ...' Mo swallowed the remains of the Mars Bar. 'Well – it's important, man. I mean, all those kids getting killed.'

'While we made fortunes. And came out with a lot of sentimental shit. That's where we were wrong. You're either in the social conscience business or show business. You're just foolish if you think you can combine them like that.'

'No, man. I mean, you can say things which people will hear.'

'You say what your audience wants. A Frank Sinatra audience gets their shit rapped back to them by Frank Sinatra. Jimi Hendrix gives a Jimi Hendrix audience what they want to hear. Is that what I want to get back into?'

But Mo had lost him. Mo was watching the tattoos crawl up his arms. He said vaguely: 'You need different music for different moods. There's nothing wrong with the New Riders, say, if you're trying to get off some paranoia trip. And you get up on Hendrix. That's what it's like. Like uppers and downers, you know.'

'Okay,' said Jimi. 'You're right. But it's the other stuff that's stupid. Why do they always want you to keep saying things? If you're just a musician that's all you should have to be. When you're playing a gig, anyway, or making a record. Anything else should come out of that. If you wanna do benefits, free concerts, okay. But your opinions should be private. They want to turn us into politicians.'

'I tol' you,' said Mo, staring intensely at his arms. 'Nobody asks that. You do what you want to do.'

'Nobody asks it, but you always feel you got to give it to 'em.' Jimi rolled over and lay on his back, scratching his head. 'Then you blame them for it.'

'Not everyone thinks they owe anything to anyone,' said Mo mildly as his skin undulated over his flesh.

'Maybe that's it,' said Jimi. 'Maybe that's what kills you. Jesus Christ. Psychologically, man, you know, that means you must be in one hell of a mess. Jesus Christ. That's suicide, man. Creepy.'

'They killed you,' said Mo.

'No, man. It was suicide.'

Mo watched the world snake crawl. Could this Hendrix be an imposter?

CHAPTER SIX

'So what you going to do, then?' said Mo. They were on the road to Skye and running low on fuel.

'I was a cunt to come back,' said Jimi. 'I thought I had some kind of duty.'

Mo shrugged. 'Maybe you have, you know.'

'And maybe I haven't.'

'Sure.' Mo saw a filling station ahead. The gauge read Empty and a red light was flashing on the panel. It always happened like that. He'd hardly ever been stranded. He glanced in the mirror and saw his own mad eyes staring back at him. Momentarily he wondered if he should turn the mirror a little to see if Jimi's reflection was there too. He pushed the thought away. More paranoia. He had to stay on top of it.

While the attendant was filling the truck, Mo went to the toilet. Among the more common bits of graffiti on the wall was the slogan 'Hawkwind is Ace.' Maybe Jimi was right. Maybe his day was over and he should have stayed dead. Mo felt miserable. Hendrix had been his only hero. He did up his flies and the effort drained off the last of his energy. He staggered against the door and began to slide down towards the messy floor. His mouth was dry; his heart was thumping very fast. He tried to remember how many pills he'd swallowed recently. Maybe he was about to O.D.

He put his hands up to the door-handle and hauled himself to his feet. He bent over the lavatory bowl and shoved his finger down his throat. Everything was moving. The bowl was alive. A greedy mouth trying to swallow him. The walls heaved and moved in on him. He heard a whistling noise. Nothing came up. He stopped trying to vomit, turned, steadied himself as best as he could, brushed aside the little white stick men who tried to grab at him, dragged the door open and plunged through. Outside, the attendant was putting the cap back on the tank. He wiped his big hands on a piece of rag and put the rag back into his overalls, saying something. Mo found some money in his back pocket and gave it to him. He heard a voice:

'You okay, laddie?'

The man had offered him a genuine look of concern.

Mo mumbled something and clambered into the cab.

The man ran up as Mo started the engine, waving money and green stamps.

'What?' said Mo. He managed to wind the window down. The man's face changed to a malevolent devil's mask. Mo knew enough not to worry about it. 'What?'

He thought he heard the attendant say: 'Your friend's already paid.'

'That's right, man,' said Jimi from beside him.

'Keep it,' said Mo. He had to get on the road quickly. Once he was driving he would be more in control of himself. He fumbled a cartridge at random from the case. He jammed it into the slot. The tape started halfway through a Stones album. Jagger singing *Let it Bleed* had a calming effect on Mo. The snakes stopped winding up and down his arms and the road ahead became steady and clearer. He'd never liked the Stones much. A load of wankers, really, though you had to admit Jagger had a style of his own which no one could copy. But basically wankers like the rest of the current evil-trippers, like Morrison and Alice Cooper. It occurred to him he was wasting his time thinking about nothing but bands, but what else was there to think about? Anyway how else could you see your life? The mystical thing didn't mean much to him. Scientology was a load of crap. At any rate, he couldn't see anything in it. The guys running all that stuff seemed to be more hung-up than the people they were supposed to be helping. That was true of a lot of things. Most people who told you they wanted to help you were getting off on you in some way. He'd met pretty much every kind of freak by now. Sufis, Hare Krishnas, Jesus Freaks, Meditators, Processors, Divine Lighters. They could all talk better than him, but they all seemed to need more from him than they could give. You get into people when you were tripping. Acid had done a lot for him that way. He could suss out the hype-merchants so easily these days. And by that test Jimi couldn't be a fake. Jimi was straight. Fucked up now, possibly, but okay.

The road was long and white and then it became a big boulder. Mo couldn't tell if the boulder was real or not. He drove at it, then changed his mind, braking sharply. A red car behind him swerved and hooted as it went past him through the boulder which disappeared. Mo shook all over. He took out the Stones tape and changed it for the Grateful Dead's *American Beauty*, turned down low.

'You okay, man?' said Hendrix.

'Sure. Just a bit shakey.' Mo started the Merc up.

'You want to stop and get some sleep.'

'I'll see how I feel later.'

It was sunset when Jimi said: 'We seem to be heading south.'

'Yeah,' said Mo. 'I need to get back to London.'

'You got to score?'

'Yeah.'

'Maybe I'll come in with you this time.'
'Yeah?'
'Maybe I won't.'

CHAPTER SEVEN

By the time Mo had hitched to the nearest tube station and reached Ladbroke Grove he was totally wasted. The images were all inside his head now: pictures of Jimi from the first time he'd seen him on TV playing *Hey, Joe* (Mo had still been at school then), pictures of Jimi playing at Woodstock, at festivals and gigs all over the country. Jimi in big, feathered hats, bizarre multi-coloured shirts, several rings on each finger, playing that white Strat, flinging the guitar over his head, plucking the strings with his teeth, shoving it under his straddled legs, making it wail and moan and throb, doing more with a guitar than anyone had done before. Only Jimi could make a guitar come alive in that way, turning the machine into an organic creature, simultaneously a prick, a woman, a white horse, a sliding snake. Mo glanced at his arms, but they were still. The sun was beginning to set as he turned into Lancaster Road, driven more by a mixture of habit and momentum than any energy or sense of purpose. He had another image in his head now, of Jimi as a soul thief, taking the energy away from the audience. Instead of a martyr, Jimi became the vampire. Mo knew that the paranoia was really setting in and the sooner he got hold of some uppers the better. He couldn't blame Jimi for how he felt. He hadn't slept for two days. That was all it was. Jimi had given everything to the people in the audience, including his life. How many people in the audience had died for Jimi?

He crawled up the steps of the house in Lancaster Road and rang the third bell down. There was no answer. He was shaking badly. He held on to the concrete steps and tried to calm himself, but it got worse and he thought he was going to pass out.

The door behind him opened.

'Mo?'

It was Dave's chick, Jenny, wearing a purple brocade dress. Her hair was caked with wet henna.

'Mo? You all right?'

Mo swallowed and said: 'Hullo, Jenny. Where's Dave?'

'He went down the Mountain Grill to get something to eat. About half an hour ago. Are you all right, Mo?'

'Tired. Dave got any uppers?'

'He had a lot of mandies in.' Mo accepted the news.

'Can you let me have a couple of quids' worth?'

'You'd better ask him yourself, Mo. I don't know who he's promised them to.'

Mo nodded and got up carefully.

'You want to come in and wait, Mo?' said Jenny.

Mo shook his head. 'I'll go down the Mountain. See you later, Jenny.'

'See you later, Mo. Take care, now.'

Mo shuffled slowly up Lancaster Road and turned the corner into Portobello Road. He thought he saw the black and chrome Merc cross the top of the street. The buildings were all crowding in on him. He saw them grinning at him, leering. He heard them talking about him. There were fuzz everywhere. A woman threw something at him. He kept going until he reached the Mountain Grill and had stumbled through the door. The cafe was crowded with freaks but there was nobody there he knew. They all had evil, secretive expressions and they were whispering.

'You fuckers,' he mumbled, but they pretended they weren't listening. He saw Dave.

'Dave? Dave, man!'

Dave looked up, grinning privately. 'Hi, Mo. When did you get back to town?' He was dressed in new, clean denims with fresh patches on them. One of the patches said 'Star Rider'.

'Just got in.' Mo leaned across the tables, careless of the intervening people, and whispered in Dave's ear. 'I hear you got some mandies.'

Dave's face became serious. 'Sure. Now?'

Mo nodded.

Dave rose slowly and paid his bill to the dark, fat lady at the till. 'Thanks, Maria.'

Dave took Mo by the shoulder and led him out of the café. Mo wondered if Dave was about to finger him. He remembered that Dave had been suspected more than once.

Dave said softly as they went along. 'How many d'you need, Mo?'

'How much are they?'

Dave said: 'You can have them for ten p each.'

'I'll have five quids' worth. A hundred, yeah?'

'Fifty.'

They got back to Lancaster Road and Dave let himself in with two keys, a Yale and a mortise. They went up a dark, dangerous stairway. Dave's room was gloomy, thick with incense, with painted blinds covering the window. Jenny sat on a mattress in the corner listening to Ace on the stereo. She was knitting.

'Hi, Mo,' she said. 'So you found him.'

Mo sat down on the mattress in the opposite corner. 'How's it going, Jenny?' he said. He didn't like Dave, but he liked Jenny. He made a big effort to be polite. Dave was standing by a chest of drawers, dragging a box from under a pile of tasselled curtains. Mo looked past him and saw Jimi standing there. He was dressed in a hand-painted silk shirt with roses all over it. There was a jade talisman on a silver chain round his throat. He had the white Strat in his hands. His eyes were closed as he played it. Almost immediately Mo guessed he was looking at a poster.

Dave counted fifty mandies into an aspirin bottle. Mo reached into his jeans and found some money. He gave Dave a five pound note and Dave gave him the bottle. Mo opened the bottle and took out a lot of the pills, swallowing them fast. They didn't act right away, but he felt better for taking them. He got up.

'See you later, Dave.'

'See you later, man,' said Dave. 'Maybe in Finch's tonight.'

'Yeah.'

CHAPTER EIGHT

Mo couldn't remember how the fight started. He'd been sitting quietly in a corner of the pub drinking his pint of bitter when that big fat fart who was always in there causing trouble decided to pick on him. He remembered getting up and punching the fat fart. There had been a lot of confusion then and he had somehow knocked the fat fart over the bar. Then a few people he knew pulled him away and took him back to a basement in Oxford Gardens where he listened to some music.

It was *Band of Gipsies* that woke him up. Listening to *Machine Gun* he realized suddenly that he didn't like it. He went to the pile of records and found other Hendrix albums. He played *Are You Experienced*, the first album, and *Electric*

Ladyland, and he liked them much better. Then he played *Band of Gipsies* again.

He looked round the dark room. Everyone seemed to be totally spaced out.

'He died at the right time,' he said. 'It was over for him, you know. He shouldn't have come back.'

He felt in his pocket for his bottle of mandies. There didn't seem to be that many left. Maybe someone had ripped them off in the pub. He took a few more and reached for the bottle of wine on the table, washing them down. He put *Are You Experienced* on the deck again and lay back. 'That was really great,' he said. He fell asleep. He shook a little bit. His breathing got deeper and deeper. When he started to vomit in his sleep nobody noticed. By that time everyone was right out of it. He choked quietly and then stopped.

CHAPTER NINE

About an hour later a black man came into the room. He was tall and elegant. He radiated energy. He wore a white silk shirt and white jeans. There were shiny patent leather boots on his feet. A chick started to get up as he came into the room. She looked bemused.

'Hi,' said the newcomer. 'I'm looking for Shakey Mo. We ought to be going.'

He peered at the sleeping bodies and then looked closer at one which lay a little apart from the others. There was vomit all over his face and over his shirt. His skin was a ghastly, dirty green. The black man stepped across the others and knelt beside Mo, feeling his heart, taking his pulse.

The chick stared stupidly at him. 'Is he all right?'

'He's O-D'ed,' the newcomer said quietly. 'He's gone. D'you want to get a doctor or something, honey?'

'Oh, Jesus,' she said.

The black man got up and walked to the door.

'Hey,' she said. 'You look just like Jimi Hendrix, you know that?'

'Sure.'

'You can't be – you're not, are you? I mean, Jimi's dead.'

Jimi shook his head and smiled his old smile. 'Shit, lady. They can't kill Jimi.' He laughed as he left.

The chick glanced down at the small, ruined body covered

in its own vomit. She swayed a little, rubbing at her thighs. She frowned. Then she went as quickly as she could from the room, hampered by her long cotton dress, and into the street. It was nearly dawn and it was cold. The tall figure in the white shirt and jeans didn't seem to notice the cold. It strode up to the big Mercedes camper parked near the end of the street.

The chick began to run after the black truck as it started up and rolled a little way before it had to stop on the red light at the Ladbroke Grove intersection.

'Wait,' she shouted. 'Jimi!'

But the camper was moving before she could reach it.

She saw it heading north towards Kilburn.

She wiped the clammy sweat from her face. She must be freaking. She hoped when she got back to the basement that there wouldn't really be a dead guy there.

She didn't need it.

THE GREATER CONQUEROR

CHAPTER ONE

He felt he was much more than one man. Not one god, even, but many ... There seemed to be a hundred other entities writhing within him. Writhing to release themselves. Every limb, every projection of bone seemed to be part of another being.

He lay on the fur-strewn bed, sweating, dominated by movement in his mind and body which he was incapable of controlling. Alexander the Great groaned in torment.

The buxom Corinthian woman spat into the rushes on the floor of the tavern.

'That for the God-King!'

But the silence around her put a stop to her enlarging the theme. The Thracian known as Simon of Byzantium lifted his bronze cup, the sleeve of his silk-trimmed jerkin falling back down his bronze arm, and sucked sweet Persian wine into his throat. He sensed the discomfort the other roisterers felt towards the woman and, because he could be cautious, dropped his arm from her thick waist and pushed her from him.

He looked down his long nose. His scarred face moved and he smiled as he addressed an old Persian soldier.

'You say you were in the army Darius led against Alexander?'

'That's right – a charioteer. His cavalry ran rings round us.'

'What did *you* think of him?'

'Alexander? I don't know. I was quite close to him at one stage and saw a spearman get a blow at him – struck him in the thigh. He yelled – not in pain but when he saw his own blood flowing. He couldn't believe it. For a short time he was an open target as he stared down at his thigh, dabbing at the blood with his finger and inspecting it. Then he shouted something – I didn't recognize the language – and was in command of himself again. They said the wound healed unnaturally quickly.'

'He claims to be the son of Zeus,' the Corinthian woman said from the shadows, 'but many Persians say he's evil Ahriman's spawn.'

Simon pursed his lips and fingered his wine cup. 'Perhaps he's just a mortal,' he suggested, 'a mortal of unusual vitality?'

'Perhaps,' the Persian soldier said. 'I only know he's conquered the world.'

'I heard he halted his Indian campaign at the River Indus – why should he do that?' Simon said.

'His Macedonians say they forced him to stop, but I cannot believe that. Even Alexander must tire – that's my theory. I think he needed to rest and recuperate. Throughout his campaigns he's hardly slept; must move on continually as if driven to conquer. Who knows what spurred him to conquest – or what made him put a temporary halt to his victories?'

'The Indians have an ancient and mighty religion of which we know little,' said a middle-aged and scrawny trader from Carthage. 'Could their Gods be stronger than ours? Stronger than Alexander?' He pulled at his grey-streaked beard. His many rings glinted in the ill-lit place.

'Such talk is heresy these days,' cautioned the Persian, but it could be seen that he was contemplating this idea.

'People talk of nothing but the Macedonian,' said the swarthy trader. 'From the Bosphorus to the Nile they curse or praise him. But what is he other than a man who has been lucky? Events have shaped him, not he them. He owes much to his foresighted father King Philip, and that warped mother Queen Olympias, both of whom, in their separate ways, prepared the world for his conquests. What reason for instance did he have for his meanderings in Persia some years ago? Why, instead of pressing on, did he embark on a wild goose chase after Darius? He had no reason save that events were not ready for him.'

'I like to think this of great men, also.' Simon smiled. 'But I would join his army for my own convenience.'

'So that's why you're in Babylon. I wondered about you, my friend. Where are you from?' The Carthaginian poured himself more wine from a skin.

'I was born in Thrace, but I'm Byzantine by adoption. I've spent seven years there as Captain of Infantry. But now I've the urge to see the East and since Alexander goes East, decided to attach myself to his army. I hear he's in Babylon now?'

'That's true. But you might find him hard to meet – obviously he is not personally concerned with the hiring of mercenaries.' The Persian's tone was friendly.

'I've heard this man – or God – spoken of so often that I've a mind to meet him if that's possible.'

'Good luck to you, friend. He'll either kill you or promote you. He's a man of extremes.'

'Are not all great conquerors?'

'You're marvellous learned for a mercenary.' The Carthaginian grinned.

Simon picked up his scabbarded short-sword from the bench.

'And you're marvellous curious, friend. Know you not that all Arts are encouraged in Byzantium, just as they were in ancient Greece – including the Arts of Reading and Philosophy.'

The Persian laughed. 'That's the story Byzantium tells. I for one do not believe that any city could be so enlightened. All you Westerners yearn for a Greece that never was – your whole philosophy is based on a need for perfection; a perfection you can never attain because it never existed. Believe me, the gutters of Byzantium still stink!'

'Not so strongly as Persian jealousy,' Simon said, and left before he was called upon to take the argument to its conclusion.

But behind him in the tavern the Persian had not been angered. Instead he was laughing, wiping his mouth with his arm stump.

Simon heard the laughter as he crossed the dim Square of the Bazaar, almost deserted of merchants and customers. The sun was still setting. It was nearly curfew. A few merchants baling their goods looked up as he strode, a tall, gaunt, fighting man, in smooth old leather, towards the Street of the Bronzeworkers where he had a friend.

Around him, golden Babylon squatted like an ancient monster, containing all knowledge, all secrets, her stepped houses, palaces, and temples soaking the last of the sun into their burnished hides. He walked up the steeply rising street and came at length to a small white house without windows. He knocked.

For a while he waited patiently as darkness came. Eventually bolts were withdrawn on the other side of the door and it was opened. An eye gleamed. The door opened wider.

Wizened Hano smiled welcomingly. 'Come in, Simon. So you reached our splendid Babylon!'

Simon stepped into the house. It was very dark, over-hot, with the unpleasantly bitter smell of metal. The old Phoenician clutched at his arm and led him down the dark passage.

'Will you be staying in Babylon, my boy?' Hano said, and then, before Simon could answer this question: 'How's the sword?'

'I intend to see Alexander,' Simon said, disliking the old man's touch though he liked Hano greatly. 'And the sword is excellent, has kept its edge in a dozen fights – I intend to hire it to Alexander.'

Hano's grip tightened as they entered a dark, smoky room, a red brazier gleaming in its centre. Around the smoke-stained walls were weapons – swords, shields, lances – and several couches and small tables were scattered on the floor. The smoke caught in Simon's lungs and he coughed it out. Hano pointed to a couch. 'Sit down, Simon.' He shuffled towards his own couch on the other side of the brazier, stretched himself at full length and scratched his hooked nose.

'Alexander has many swords.'

'I know – but if you granted me a favour it might facilitate my meeting him.'

'I owe you friendship and more,' Hano said, 'for you saved me from an unpleasant death that time in Thebes nine years ago. But though I sense what you want of me I am reluctant to agree to it.'

'Why?'

'An old man's caution, maybe, but the stories I've been hearing of late have been disquieting. Alexander claims himself son of Zeus, Jupiter Ammon. Others say that the Persian evil one Ahriman possesses him. All or none of this may be true – but every oracle from here to Pela is prophesying turmoil and trouble for the world and the king who rules it. Perhaps you would be wiser to join some ordinary caravan travelling east?' Hano pulled back his woollen robe, revealing a pale and unlovely leg. He poised his wrinkled hand and then almost hurled it at a spot on his leg and began to scratch at the place with his talons of nails.

'I'm sick of this prattle of gods and demons. Can no one be content simply to believe in men and what men could be if they ceased blaming their misfortunes on unseen gods rather than on their own ineffectiveness? Life's not easy, it is a hard task to live it well and with grace – but, by Hades, let's not complicate it with deities and water-nymphs!'

Simon spat into the brazier which flared and spluttered.

Hano scratched at his thigh, drawing back more of his robe to do so, revealing a greater expanse of unhealthy flesh.

'I have seen supernatural manifestations of evil, my boy.'

'You have seen what a muddled brain wished you to see.'

'What matter? Now, let's end this conversation before you yell more heresies and have us both arrested.'

'Heresy and treason combined if Alexander's chest-puffing claim be true.' Simon looked away from the old man's thin legs and stared into the brazier.

Hano changed the subject.

'In Utopia,' he said to Simon, 'you'd yet be seeking further perfection. You call yourself a realist, Simon – perfection is not a reality.'

'Realities can be created,' said Simon.

'True,' Hano agreed. 'But by the same logic, realities can be made unreal – unrealities made real. What if there *were* supernatural beings. How would you fit them into your theory?'

'The situation will never arise.'

'Let us hope so.'

The Phoenician turned his old twisted face towards Simon. The brazier light stained it a reddish brown, showing the wrinkles of mingled cynicism, fatalism, and good nature. Hano said at length: 'Very well.'

He got up and moved about the crowded room taking a pot from one shelf, a skin of wine from another.

Soon the smell of herbs came from the pot on the brazier as Hano brewed wine for his guest.

'You'll help.' Simon said.

'Alexander owes me a favour. But he has strange ways of repaying debts and I'd not normally be foolish enough to remind him of this one.'

'What did you do for him?'

'Set the handle of a star-metal blade with black opals.'

'That was a favour!' Simon laughed.

Hano scowled, but genially. 'Know you not what that meant? It meant he could not directly handle iron or anything likely to conduct its force to his body. Black opal is one of the few gems which will serve to negate the flow.'

'So?'

'So Alexander has a weakness. Iron will harm him.'

'If I had such a secret I would kill the man who held it.' Simon said reflectively.

'Not if you were Alexander and the man was dear to Olympias.'

'*You* know Queen Olympias!'

'Olympias wishes me kept alive so I can feed her with secrets.'

'Dark secrets, I'll warrant, if the stories of her are half-true.'

'They do not touch the real truth about her.'

'Does she really sport with snakes at these rites?'

'Aye – and black goats are present too.'

Simon swore.

Hano handed him a cup of hot wine. As he drank he said: 'I'm impatient to meet the God-King – how will you help?'

'I'll give you a letter and a token to take to Alexander. But be wary, my boy. Be wary.'

CHAPTER TWO

Though he rarely admitted it, the idea of a supernatural world of gods and spirits disturbed Simon. Had it been practicable he might have become a militant atheist but instead he kept his opinions secret for the most part and did his utmost not to question them or even think of them.

When he reached the great golden palace of Alexander he paused and stared up at it with admiration. It was illuminated by hundreds of torches many of which, on long poles, surrounded the palace. Others flared on its many ramparts.

Two guards came forward. They were Babylonians in high helmets with oiled hair and beards. Their javelins threatened him.

In poor Babylonian Simon said:

'I come to see King Alexander – I have a token and a letter for him.'

They treated him with some respect, though they divested him of his sword and led him to the main gate where, after conversation he was admitted.

He was made to wait several times, being studied and questioned by a variety of viziers and minions of the king, but at last he was ushered into a large chamber.

Big windows let in the flickering torchlight. A great bed of brass, silver, and gold, heaped with silks and furs, was in the centre of the room.

Alexander was sitting up in bed. He had been sweating, Simon could see. His nose told him the same story.

The odour, in fact was bad. Far worse than ordinary perspiration. Simon couldn't place the smell.

With a degree of nervousness Simon approached the huge bed.

Suddenly, King Alexander grinned and stuck out a handsome hand.

'You have a letter for me, I hear – and a token?'

'I have, sire.' Simon gave the letter and the little talisman to Alexander, studying the king's strange face. In a way it was boyish; in another ancient and sensuous. He had a long nose and thick lips, heavily lidded eyes, and brown, curly hair. Simon was taken aback by the king's lack of ceremony, by his friendly grin. Was this the God-King? The spawn of evil?

Alexander read the letter quickly, nodding to himself.

'Did Hano tell you of my debt to him?'

'No, sire,' Simon said tactfully.

'He has many secrets, Hano – but he's an old man and, in his generosity, keeps few to himself, I've heard.'

'He seems curiously tight-lipped, sire,' Simon replied, anxious for his friend's life, 'and even I who saved his life one time in Thebes can never get a full reply to any question I ask him.'

Alexander looked up sharply, staring Simon in the face with peculiarly wide eyes.

'So you wish to join my army. Hano recommends you as a fighting man – suggests you join my staff. I choose my officers with care, Simon of Byzantium.'

'I wish only a trial, sire.'

'You shall have it.'

Alexander studied the letter again.

'You're from Byzantium, I note. My father Philip was repulsed by that city some years ago – but that does not mean I can have no love for the city – perhaps the contrary. It's well known I disliked him and can admire a city which withstood his attack.' Alexander smiled again. 'Though she did not hold out for long against Philip's son, did she?'

'No, sire.'

Alexander had an almost tangible vitality, but he was evidently unwell. This ailment was not solely confined to his body, either, Simon felt.

Alexander mused, caressing the little amulet.

'I have need of a herald – a man who can travel between wherever I am campaigning and the capital of Macedonia.'

'I thought Persia was your base these days, sire.'

'You've been listening to Greek and Macedonian criticism, no doubt. They say I've forsaken my own lands for the fleshpots and honours of the East. That's a lie. It is too far to travel back always to Pela. Persia offers a better base for my operations. There are still a few acres of the world left for me to conquer, Simon – and they all lie eastwards.'

Alexander sank back into his silks, eyeing the Thracian.

'You'll serve my mother and myself as a messenger.'

Simon put his hand to his lips and said courteously: 'I had rather hoped to go with the army, sire.'

Alexander frowned slightly. 'And so you will, of course. No doubt there'll be fighting for you – and new knowledge. I'm pleased that you're literate. Most of my captains are chosen for several qualities – courage, loyalty – and learning. You appear to have courage and learning – but I must find out about your loyalty, you understand.'

Simon nodded. 'That is logical, sire.'

'Good, then –' Alexander broke off as the doors of the chamber opened behind Simon. The Thracian turned to stare at the door.

A vizier, in long cloth-of-gold robes, hurried into the room. He prostrated himself before the king's bed.

'Son of Zeus,' he mumbled, 'a message.'

'Is it secret?'

'No, sire – they say it is already common knowledge.'

'Then speak – what is it?' Alexander propped himself into a sitting position again.

'A massacre, sire – in Lonarten – a troop of your Macedonian horse went berserk, killed many hundreds of women and children. There are rumours of cannibalism and unhealthy rites ...' The vizier stopped as a smile crossed Alexander's sensuous lips. 'The people are asking for your interference – for compensation.'

Alexander smiled again. Simon was sickened by the sight. The king could be seen to grip hold of the bed-clothes as if attempting to control himself. He groaned once, slightly.

With effort he said: 'We must call a halt to – we must stop . . .' Then he flung back his handsome head and bellowed with laughter. It was a laughter totally evil, a horrible, malicious joy which seethed around the room, echoing and roaring in Simon's horrified ears.

'Seize the complainers,' Alexander shouted, 'we'll sell them as eunuchs to the harems of Turkey. Teach them that the ways of a god are not the ways of a mere king – teach them not to question the word or actions of the Son of Zeus!'

Hurriedly, the vizier backed out of the room.

Simon, forgetful for his own safety, leaned forward and shouted into Alexander's twisted face:

'You are mad – for your own sake do not let this massacre continue. Your unruly troops will cause a revolution – you will lose your empire.'

Alexander's eyes opened even wider. A hand leapt from the silks and furs and seized Simon's ear. The mouth curled and even teeth moved as Alexander snarled:

'For you I will *invent* a death!'

Simon grasped the wrist attempting to wrest himself from Alexander's grip. He was sickened, trembling and shaken by the strength in one so evidently ill. He felt the presence of something more than common insanity. What had changed the pleasant, practical soldier into this manifestation of evil? How could such different qualities exist in one body? Terror clouded his mind.

With a wrench he was free of the king's grasp and backed panting away from him.

'They said you were Ahriman's spawn – and I did not believe them,' he gasped.

Alexander grimaced, flung back the bed-clothes and leapt to the ground, advancing towards Simon, with hands outstretched.

'I am Zeus's son – born of god and mortal to rule the world. Abase yourself, heretic, for I have the power to send you to Hades!'

'All men have that power,' Simon said, turned and ran for the great doors, tugged them open and, before he could be stopped fled down the shouting corridors, blind to everything but the need to escape from the screaming madman behind him.

He remembered little of the flight, of the two fights, in the first of which he somehow gained a weapon, of his breathless running through the streets of Babylon with hordes of soldiers seeking him out.

He ran.

He had run himself virtually to death when several warriors pinned him in a blind alley and he turned, snarling like an animal to defend himself. Crouching, sword raised, he waited for them as they cautiously advanced.

They had not expected such ferocity. He had cut the first soldier down in a trice and sliced the flesh from another's arm.

In front of him, as if superimposed on the real scene before him, was the great, sensuous head of Alexander still roaring with crazy laughter.

Simon had seen madmen many times. But Alexander had more than madness. He slashed with his sword and missed his target, fell forward, rolled on his back, brought his sword across his face to deflect a blade which had hurtled down through the confused night. He edged back, flung himself sideways, slashing, scrambled up and brought the edge of his sword up to chop a man's jugular.

Then he was running again, every limb aching, but a terrible fear, a fear of more than death or torture, driving, driving him onward to escape.

When the silent, dark-robed men appeared out of the night and surrounded him he cut at one but his sword seemed to meet metal, his hand went numb and the blade fell to the stones of the streets.

Alexander's face rose before him, laughing, laughing. The roaring, evil merriment filled his head, then his whole body until it seemed that he, Simon, was Alexander, that he was enjoying the bloody joke, the evil, malignant glee pouring wildly from his shaking body.

Then peace of a kind, and hazy, mysterious dreams where he saw strange shapes moving through the smoke from a million red and glowing braziers.

Simon felt a hard, smooth surface beneath his back.

He opened his eyes warily.

A lean, white, thin-lipped face looked kindly down at him.

'I am Abaris,' he said.

'Simon of Byzantium,' said the Thracian.

'You have witnessed darkness?' It was only half a question.

'Yes,' Simon replied, bemused.

'We are men of light. The Magi welcome you. You are safe here.'

'Magi? They are priests in Persia – but you're not Persian.'

'That is so.'

'Abaris? There is an Abaris of legend – a wizard, was he not – a priest of Apollo who rode on an arrow?'

The Magi made no reply to this, simply smiled.

'You have incurred the wrath of Alexander. How long would you say you had to live?'

'A strange question. I'd say as long as my wits were sharp enough to evade the searchings of his soldiers.'

'You would be wrong.'

Simon pushed himself upright on the wide bench and looked around him. Two other priests sat regarding him from across the bare room. Daylight filtered in from a hole in the ceiling.

'Do I really owe you my life?'

'We think you do – but you are in no debt. We wish we could give such concrete aid to all enemies of Alexander.'

'I am not his enemy – he is mine.'

'You have witnessed what he is – can you still say that?'

Simon nodded. 'I am his enemy,' he agreed and then amended this with: 'Or at least the enemy of what he represents.'

'You are exact – we also are the enemies of what Alexander represents.'

Simon put his head on one side and smiled slightly. 'Ah – let us be careful. He is insane, that is all. He represents material evil, not supernatural.'

Briefly, Abaris looked impatiently away, frowning. Then his features resumed their earlier look.

'It is a bold thing to be an unbeliever in these times.'

'Bold or not – it is what I am.' Simon swung his legs off the bench. He felt incredibly weak.

Abaris said: 'We Magi worship Ormuzd. Simply – Alexander represents Ahriman.'

'These are the twin facets of your single deity are they not?' Simon said. He nodded. 'I know a little about your cult – it's cleaner than most. You worship Fire, Sun, and Light – with a minimum of ritual.'

'True. A man who is confident in his soul needs little ritual.'

Simon was satisfied by this.

'We would be grateful if you would ally yourself with us, the Magi,' Abaris said quietly. 'In return we will protect you from Alexander's minions as best we can.'

'I told you – and I do not wish to seem ungrateful – my wits will keep me safe from the Macedonian's warriors.'

'We refer to his supernatural minions.'

Simon shook his head. 'I respect your beliefs – but I cannot accept them personally.'

Abaris leaned forward and said urgently, softly:

'Simon, you must aid us. Alexander and his mother are both possessed. For years we have been aware of this. For years we have attempted to fight the forces possessing them – and we are losing. You have seen how Ahriman controls Alexander. You must aid us!'

Simon said: 'You have cloaked the simple fact of Alexander's madness in a shroud of supernatural speculation.'

Abaris shook his head, saying nothing. Simon continued:

'I have seen many men go mad with riches and power – Alexander is another. When he dies his good works will survive but the evil will be eliminated by time.'

'You are naïve, young man. Why, Achilles believed that...' Abaris bit his lip and lapsed into silence.

'Achilles? He died a thousand years ago. How do you know what he believed?'

Abaris turned away. 'Of course, I could not know,' he said. His eyes were hooded.

'You give me cause to think you really are the Abaris of legend,' Simon smiled. He was joking. But even to his ears the joke rang true.

Abaris said: 'Can a man live for more than a thousand years?'

'No,' Simon said, 'no.' He said it almost savagely, for it was what he wished to believe.

Out there, in a palace of Babylon, there was *evil*, he thought. But it was not, could not be – *must* not be supernatural.

Abaris now said:

'Alexander has reigned almost thirteen years – a mystic number. Our oracles prophesied that the turning point would come after thirteen years of rule. Now, as we fear, Alexander and the forces which act through him will bring an unchecked reign of evil to the world – or else, and the chance is small, he will be stopped.'

'You wish me to aid you in this. I must dissent. To help you I would have to believe you – that I cannot do.'

Abaris seemed to accept this. When he next spoke it was in a detached, trancelike voice.

'Ahriman – the multiplicity of Ahrimans whom we designate by the one name – selected Olympias many years ago. He needed a vessel through which to work and, at that time, no mortal had been born who would serve Ahriman's purpose. So he took possession of poor Olympias. Philip, that great and wronged man, went regularly to the Isle of Samothrace on pilgrimage and, one year, Olympias made it her business to be there also. A love potion was all she needed. Philip was enamoured of her. They had a son – Alexander...'

Simon said wearily: 'This is mere gossip such as old women make in the markets.'

'Ormuzd protect you if you ever learn the truth,' was all Abaris said.

Simon rose shakily. 'If there is anything I can do to repay you – some material act, perhaps – I am very willing.'

Abaris thought for a moment. Then he took a scroll from his robe. He unrolled it and glanced over the weird script. It was not Persian, Simon knew, but what it was he could not tell.

Abaris handed the scroll to Simon. 'We'll furnish you with a horse and a disguise. Will you go to Pela for us? Will you deliver a message to our brothers?'

'Willingly,' Simon said, though he was aware that to journey to the capital of Macedonia would be courting danger.

'They live in secret,' Abaris told Simon, 'but we will tell you how to find them. Also we will furnish you with weapons, a horse and a disguise of some sort.'

'I'd be grateful for that,' Simon smiled.

'We'll give you a day for resting and allowing the herbs we'll give you to drink to do their work – then you can start off.

You should have little trouble here, for our magic will protect you and we know a secret way out of the city.'

Simon lay back on the bench. 'Healing herbs will be very welcome,' he said, 'and something to help me take a dreamless sleep . . .'

CHAPTER THREE

Outside, the courtiers glanced at one another, not daring to enter the room where a man groaned.

A short, clever-looking man in ornate war-gear turned to a calm-faced, sensitive man.

'Why was he so anxious to apprehend the Thracian, I wonder, Anaxarchus?'

The sensitive man shook his head. 'I have no idea. I hear he was from my home city, Abdera, before he went to Byzantium. For all my people say that the folk of Abdera are stupid, some very clever men were born there.'

'And you, of course, are one,' the soldier smiled ironically.

'I must be – I am philosopher attached to Alexander's train,' Anaxarchus said.

The warrior took several nervous paces up the corridor, wheeled around, cursing. 'By the Salamander's breath, are we never to finish our conquests? What is wrong with Alexander, Anaxarchus? How long has he been like this? Rumours came to Egypt, but I discounted them.'

'He is ill, Ptolemy, that is all,' Anaxarchus said, but he did not believe his own words.

'That is *all*! Even if I had not heard the Oracle of Libya speak of terrible strifings in this world and the others I would be troubled. Things are happening. Anaxarchus – doom-clouds are covering the world.'

'Gloomy, Ptolemy – he is only sick. He has a fever.'

Another awful groan came from behind the doors, a terrified and terrible groan of awful agony. Neither did it seem to represent physical pain but some deeper agony of spirit.

'An unusual fever,' Ptolemy said savagely. He strode towards the doors, but Anaxarchus blocked his passage.

'No, Ptolemy – you would not emerge with your sanity intact, I warn you.'

Ptolemy looked at the scholar for a moment, then turned and almost ran down the corridor.

Inside the locked room, the man – or god – groaned terribly. It was as if the bones of his face were breaking apart to form individual beings. What was he? Even he could not be sure. For years he had been certain of his own power, confident that his greatness was his own. But now, it was obvious to him, poor, tormented Alexander, that he was nothing – nothing but a vessel, an agent through which many forces worked – and even those forces were united under a common name. He knew then also, that they had entered many others in the past that, if his strength broke, they would enter many more until their work was done.

Part of him begged for death.

Part of him attempted to fight that which was in him.

Part of him planned – crime.

Simon, cloaked and armed, clamped his knees against his steed's back and galloped over the sparsely-covered plains of Babylon, the folds of his cloak flying behind him like the wings of a stooping hawk.

The horse snorted, its sturdy legs flashing, its eyes big and its heart pounding.

For two hours, Simon had ridden in safety.

But now the cold night air above him was alive with dreadful sounds.

He drew his sword from its scabbard and rode on, telling himself that the noises were the flapping wings of vultures.

Then a shape came swooping in front of him. He caught a glimpse of a pale, human face. But it was not entirely human. Snakes twined on its head, blood dripped from its eyes. The horse came to a sudden halt, reared whinnying.

Simon closed his eyes against the sight.

'The herbs the Magi gave me have induced visions,' he told himself aloud in shaking tones.

But he could not believe it. He had seen them.

The Eumenides – the Furies of legend!

For the face had been that of a woman.

Now the sounds came closer, ominous. Simon urged the frightened horse onwards. Sharp female faces with serpents in place of hair, blood streaming from malevolent eyes, hands like talons, swooped and cackled about him. It was nightmare.

Then, quite suddenly, there came a dull booming sound from the distance, like the far-away sound of surf. Nearer and nearer it came until the night opened to brightness, a strange golden light which seemed to break through the blackness, splintering it into fragments. The winged creatures were caught in the glare, wheeled about uncertainly, shrieking and keening.

They were gone.

The light faded.

Simon rode on. And still he insisted to himself that what he had witnessed was hallucination. Something done to his weary brain by the potion the Magi had given him.

The rest of the night was full of nauseous sound, glimpses of things which flew or wriggled. But, convinced that he dreamed, horrified yet keeping close hold on sanity, Simon pushed the steed onwards towards Pela.

Horse and man rested for only a few hours at a time. The journey took days until, at length, eyes sunken in his head from tiredness, face grey and gaunt and mind numb he arrived at the Macedonian capital and sought out the Magi in the clay-built slums of the city.

Massiva, head of the secret order in Pela, was a tall, handsome Numidian. He greeted Simon warmly.

'We were informed of your coming and did our best, when you came close enough, to ward off the dangers which Alexander's minions sent against you.'

Simon did not reply to this. Silently, he handed over the scroll.

Massiva opened it, read it, frowning.

'This we did not know,' he said. 'Olympias has sent aid to Alexander in Babylon.'

The priest offered no explanation, so Simon did not ask for one.

Massiva shook his head wearily. 'I do not understand how one human can endure so much,' he said, 'but then she has other aid than human . . .'

'What are these stories about her?' Simon asked, thinking that he might at last find some truth where before he had heard nothing but rumour and hints.

'The simple facts concerning her activities are common knowledge here,' Massiva told him. 'She is an ardent initiate of a number of mystery cults, all worshipping the dark forces. The usual unpleasant rites, secret initiations, orgiastic celebrations. Three of the main ones, supposedly having no communication with one another, are the cults of Orpheus, Dionysius and Demeter. It's hinted that Alexander was conceived at one of these rites. In a way that is the truth – for Olympias was selected by the Dark One when she was a girl participating in the rites of a similar cult.'

Simon shook his head impatiently at this. 'I asked you for facts – not speculation.'

Massiva looked surprised. 'I indulged in no speculation, my friend. Why, the whole city lives in fear of Olympias and her friends and servants. Evil is so thick here that ordinary folk can hardly breathe for its stink.'

Simon said shortly: 'Well, I hope the information is useful to you. I've paid my debt, at least. Now, can you recommend a tavern where I can stay?'

'I can recommend none well, in this cursed city. You might try the *Tower of Cimbri*. It's comfortable, so I've heard. But be wary, take iron to bed with you.'

'I'd do that in any event,' Simon grinned, 'with Alexander after my blood and me staying in his home city.'

'You're courageous, Thracian – do not be foolish.'

'Don't worry, friend.' Simon left the house, remounted his horse and rode it towards the tavern quarter, eventually locating the *Tower of Cimbri*.

He was about to enter when he heard the sound of running from an alley which ran along the side of the building. Then a girl screamed. Drawing his sword he ran into the alley and, because he had become so hardened to sights of horror, hardly noticed the misshapen creatures menacing a frightened girl, save that they were armed and evidently powerful. The girl's eyes were round with fear and she was half-fainting. One of the twisted men put out a blunt paw to seize her, but wailed out its pain as Simon's sword caught it in the shoulder blades.

The others turned, reaching for their weapons. Simon cut two down before they could draw their swords. The fourth swung at Simon but was too clumsy. He died in a moment, his neck cloven.

Instead of thanking him, the girl stared down at the corpses in terror.

'You fool,' she muttered.

'Fool?' Simon was taken aback.

'You have killed four of Queen Olympias's retainers – did you not recognize the livery – or their kind?'

'I'm a stranger in Pela.'

'Then leave now – or be doomed.'

'No, I must see that you are safe. Quickly – I have a horse waiting in the street.' He supported her with one arm though she protested and helped her into the saddle.

He got up behind her.

'Where do you live?'

'Near the west wall – but hurry, by Hera, or they'll find the corpses and give chase.'

Following her directions, Simon guided the horse through the evening half-light.

They came to a pleasant, large house, surrounded by a garden which in turn was enclosed in high walls. They rode through the gate and she dismounted, closing them behind her. An old man appeared in the doorway to the courtyard.

'Camilla? What's happening?'

'Later, father. Have the servants stable the horse and make sure all the gates are locked – Olympias's retainers attempted to kidnap me again. This man saved me from them – but four are dead.'

'Dead? Gods!' The old man pursed his lips. He was dressed in a loose toga and had a stern, patrician face. He was evidently a nobleman, though his black-haired daughter was most unlike him.

Quickly, Simon was ushered into the house. Servants were summoned bringing bread, cheese, and fruit. He ate gratefully. As he ate he told as much of his personal story as he wished to divulge. The patrician, Merates, listened without commenting.

When Simon had finished, Merates made no direct remark but instead said, half to himself:

'If King Philip had not continued his line, there would be peace and achievement in this war-wrecked world. I curse the name of Alexander – and the she-snake who bore him. If Alexander had been left to his father's teaching, he might well have carried on the great plan of Philip. But his warped mother put different ideas into his head – turned him against his father. Now there is evil on every wind, it blows east and west, south and north – and the hounds of darkness rend, slaver, and howl in Alexander's bloody wake.'

Camilla shuddered. She had changed her street robe into a loose, diaphanous gown of blue silk. Her long, black, unbound hair fell down her back, gleaming like dark wine.

She said: 'Now, though Alexander's off on his conquests,

Olympias terrorizes Pela more than ever before. All comely youths and girls are sought out to take part in her ghastly rituals. For ten or more months she has tried to encourage me to join until, at last, her patience failed and she attempted to kidnap me. She will know that someone killed the servitors – but she need not know it was you, Simon.'

Simon nodded mutely. He found it difficult to speak as he breathed in the girl's dark beauty, intoxicated by it as he had never before been.

They were troubled times. Times of high deeds and feats of learning; times of obscene evil and wild daring. Alexander mirrored his times. With one breath he would order a massacre, with another honour a conquered city for its courage in withstanding him. His great horse Bucephalus bore his bright armoured master across the known world. Fire destroyed ancient seats of civilization, wise men were slain and innocents drowned in the flood tide of his conquests. Yet he caused new cities to be raised and libraries to be built. Men of learning followed in his train – this pupil of Aristotle – and he was an enigma to all. Greece, Persia, Babylonia, Assyria, Egypt, all fell to him. Four mighty races, four ancient civilizations bore Alexander's yoke. People had speculated on whether he was a force for darkness or enlightenment – whether he would rend the world to fragments or unite it in lasting peace. An enigma.

But now the year was 323 BC *and Alexander was aged 32. He had ruled over twelve years – soon he would have reigned thirteen . . .*

In the dark caverns of creation, existing within a multiplicity of dimensions, vital evil thrived, chuckling and plotting – crime.

For thirteen years had the forces of Light and Darkness warred in poor Alexander's soul and body, unbeknownst to the proud, grandiose and arrogant world-conqueror. But now the stars proclaimed that a certain time had come.

And Alexander suffered . . .

Riders galloped towards the corners of the world. Bright banners whipped in the wind as armies sped across the lands around the Mediterranean. Ships groaned with the weight of armoured soldiers. Blood flowed like wine and wine like water. Corpses roasted in guttering castles and the earth shook to the coming of Alexander's cavalry.

And now messengers rode to the camps of his captains, recalling them. They were needed. The final conquest was to be made. But it would not be Alexander's triumph. The triumph would belong to a greater conqueror. Some called him Ahriman.

Hastily now Alexander's captains mounted their chariots and headed towards Babylon. Many had to cross oceans, continents.

Every oracle prophesied doom – some said for Alexander, some said for the world. Never, they said, had evil clouded the world as much as now.

Ahriman had prepared the world through Alexander.

Soon the Powers of Light would be destroyed for ever and, though it might take many more centuries of completion, Ahriman could begin his plans of conquest and, finally, destruction.

There were more vehicles for his plans.

CHAPTER FOUR

Simon lazed back on a bench and ran his hand over Camilla's warm shoulders.

'Do not the heroes of legend always claim such reward from the maidens they rescue?' he asked mockingly.

She smiled at him affectionately.

'The Camilla of legend, if you remember, had nought to do with men. I've a mind to emulate her.'

'A sad waste.'

'For you, perhaps, but not for me...'

Simon pretended to sigh. 'Very well,' he said, 'I can see I shall have to wait until you eventually succumb to my undoubted attraction.'

Again she smiled. 'You have been here a week and I have not fallen yet.'

'It was good of your father to give me the position of Captain of his Bodyguard, particularly since he is risking arrest if Olympias should ever discover that I slew her servants.'

'Merates is a good and wise man,' Camilla said seriously, 'one of the few left in Pela, these days. He was close to Philip and admired him greatly. But Philip's son would have nothing to do with his father's councillors so now Merates lives in quiet retirement.'

Simon had already learnt that Camilla was the foster daughter of Merates, that she had been born to a loved and trusted Paeonian slave who had died when she was a child.

He had grown to respect the old nobleman and planned, though it was dangerous for him, to stay in Pela and probably settle there. He had already fallen in love with Camilla.

And so he courted her and although she gave him no reason to cease this courtship, on the other hand she did not encourage him overmuch. She knew him for a soldier-of-fortune and a wanderer. Perhaps she wanted to be certain of him.

But they were dark times and Simon, rationalist though he was, could not be unaware of them. He sensed the gathering storm and was restless.

One day as he was instructing a group of slaves in the art of using the shield, Merates came hurrying into the courtyard.

'Simon – a word with you.'

The Thracian propped his sword against the wall and went with Merates into the house.

There were tears in Merates's eyes when he spoke.

'Camilla is gone. She had to go on an errand in the market – a regular monthly visit to settle our score with the merchants with whom we trade. She has been gone four hours – she is normally gone one . . .'

Simon's body grew taut. 'Olympias? Do you think . . .?'

Merates nodded.

Simon turned, went swiftly to his quarters where he buckled on his leather belt bearing the scabbarded sword the Magi had given him.

He flung a blanket over his horse's back, rode it from the stable, ducking his head beneath the door beam, through the gates of the house and down the streets of Pela to the city centre.

He inquired in the market for her. She had not been seen there for well over two hours. Thinking swiftly, he headed for the slums of the city, dismounted outside a certain door and knocked.

Massiva, the black Numidian priest answered the door himself. He was dressed like a slave – evidently disguised.

'Come in, Simon. It is good to see you.'

'I wish aid, Massiva. And in return I may be able to help you.'

Massiva ushered him inside.

'What is it?'

'I am certain that Queen Olympias has kidnapped Camilla, Lord Merates's daughter.'

Massiva's expression did not change. 'It is likely – Camilla is reputed beautiful and a virgin. Olympias seeks such qualities. Either she will corrupt Camilla and force her to take an active part in the rites – or else she will make her take a passive part.'

'Passive? What do you mean?'

'The blood of virgins is needed in several spells.'

Simon shuddered.

'Can you help me? Tell me where I may find her!'

'The Rites of Cottyttia begin tonight. That is where to look.'

'Where do they take place?'

'Come, I will draw you a map. You will most likely perish in this, Simon. But you will be convinced that we have spoken truth in the past.'

Simon looked at the Negro sharply. Massiva's face was expressionless.

They called her Cotys and she was worshipped as a goddess in Thrace, Macedonia, Athens, and Corinth. For centuries her name had been connected with licentious revelry – but never had she prospered so well than in as where Queen Olympias danced with snakes in her honour. Though only part of a greater Evil One, she flourished and grew on the tormented souls of her acolytes and their victims.

The house stood on its own on a hill.

Simon recognized it from Massiva's description. It was night, silver with rime and moonlight, but there were movements in the shadows and shapes of evil portent. His breath steaming white against the darkness, Simon pressed on up the hill towards the house.

A slave greeted him as he reached the door.

'Welcome – be you *Baptae* or heretic?'

Baptae, Simon had learned from Massiva, was the name that the worshippers of Cotys called themselves.

'I come to take part in tonight's Cottyttia, that's true,' Simon said and slew the slave.

Inside the house, lighted by a single oil-lamp, Simon located the door which opened on reeking blackness. He bent and entered it and soon was creeping downwards, down into the bowels of the hill. The walls of the tunnel were slippery with clammy moss and the air was thick and difficult to breathe. The sharp sound of his sword coming from its scabbard was comforting to Simon.

His sandled feet slipped on the moss-covered stones of the passage and, as he drew nearer to his goal, his heart thudded in his rib-cage and his throat was tight for he now had something of the emotion he had felt when confronted by Alexander's insanity.

Now he heard a low chanting, half ecstatic moaning, half triumphant incantation. The sound grew louder, insinuating itself into his ears until he was caught for a moment in the terrible evil ecstasy which the Cottyttian celebrants were feeling. He controlled himself against an urge to flee, the even stronger urge to join them, and continued to advance, the rare steel sword gleaming in his fist. The iron was a comfort, at least, though he still refused to believe that there was any supernatural agency at work.

Almost tangibly the evil swirled about him as he pressed on and here his rational, doubting nature was to his advantage. Without it, he might easily have succumbed.

The chanting swelled into a great roar of evil joy and through it he heard a name being repeated over and over:

'Cotys. Cotys. Cotys. Cotys.'

He was half hypnotized by the sound, stumbled towards a curtain and wrenched it back.

He retreated a pace at what he saw.

The air was thick with incense. Golden light flared from tall black candles on an altar. From the altar rose a pillar and tied to the pillar was Camilla. She had fainted.

But it was not this that sickened him so much as the sight of the things which swarmed about the altar. They were neither men nor women but neuter. Perhaps they had once been men. They were young and good-looking, their hair long and their faces thin, the bones prominent and the eyes flickering with malignant glee. Naked, to one side of the altar, Simon saw an old woman. Her face was that of a woman of sixty, but her body seemed younger. Around it twined great serpents, caressing her. She crooned to them and led the chanting. Young women danced with the neuters, posturing and prancing.

'Cotys. Cotys. Cotys.'

The candles spurted seething light and sent shadows leaping

around the walls of the caverns. Then a peculiar golden orange brightness appeared at the top of the column to which Camilla was tied and seemed to twine and coil down the pillar.

Other shapes joined the dancing humans. Twisted shapes with great horns on their heads and the faces of beasts, the hooves of goats.

Simon moved forward, his sword held before him in instinctive protection against the evil in the cavern.

'Cease!' A name came to his lips and he shouted it out: 'In the name of Ormuzd – cease!'

A huge swelling of unhuman laughter came from the boiling brightness on the pillar and Simon saw figures form in it. Figures that were man-shaped and seemed to be at the same time part of the structure of a huge face, lined and pouched with a toothless, gaping mouth and closed eyes.

Then the eyes opened and seemed to fix themselves on Simon. The smaller figures writhed about it and it laughed again. Bile was in his throat, his head throbbed, but he gripped the sword and pushed his way through the sweating bodies of the worshippers. They grinned at him maliciously but did not attempt to stop him.

He was lost in the pull of those malicious eyes.

'Ormuzd is too weak to protect thee, mortal,' the mouth said. 'Ahriman rules here – and will soon rule the world through his vessel, Alexander.'

Still Simon pushed his way towards the pillar, towards Camilla and the leering face above her.

'Ormuzd will not aid thee, mortal. We are many and stronger. Behold me! What do you see?'

Simon made no reply. He gripped the steel blade tighter and advanced closer.

'Do you see us all? Do you see the one these revellers call Cotys? Do you see the Evil One?'

Simon staggered forwards, the last few paces between him and the entity coiling about the pillar. Olympias now pushed her face forward, the snakes hissing, their forked tongues flickering.

'Go to her, Thracian – my son knows thee – go to her and we'll have a double sacrifice. this night.'

With his free hand, Simon pushed against the scaly bodies of the snakes and sent the woman staggering back.

With trancelike deliberation he cut the bonds that held

Camilla to the pillar. But many hands, orange-gold hands, shot out from the column and gripped him in a shuddering, yet ecstatic embrace. He howled and smote at the hands and, at the touch of steel they flickered back again into their scintillating parent body.

Then he felt the clammy hands of the acolytes upon his body. Sensing that he had some advantage, Simon dragged a bunch of herbs from his shirt – herbs which Massiva had given him – and plunged them into the candle flames. A pungent aroma began to come from the flaring herbs and the naked worshippers dropped back. The apparition itself seemed to fade slightly, its light less bright.

Simon sprang at the shape, his sword flashing like silver and passing through the hazy face which snarled and laughed alternately. The sword clanged on the stone of the column. Desperately, he drew back his arm to strike another blow, his whole body weakened. He felt like an old, worn man.

'Ormuzd!' he shouted as he struck again.

Again the face snarled at him; again the golden hands shot out to embrace him so that his body thrilled with terrible weakening joy.

Then Simon felt that he was all his ancestors and a knowledge came to him, the knowledge of darkness and chaos which his forebears had possessed.

And this knowledge, though terrifying, contained within it a further knowledge – the awareness that the Forces of Darkness had been vanquished in the past and could be vanquished again.

This gave him strength. Ahriman-Cotys realized that from somewhere Simon had gained renewed energy and its shape drew in on itself, began to slide down the pillar towards Camilla.

But Simon reached her, tugged her away from the column and onto the ground. Then he drew back his arm and flung the flaming herbs into the face of the apparition.

A horrid growling sound filled the air, and, for a moment, the face faded entirely.

Simon grasped Camilla and fell back through the crowd, slashing at their naked bodies with his bright sword. Blood flowed and faces reappeared, bellowing with laughter.

Many little faces joined in the merriment, piping their mirth and detaching themselves from the greater entity to fall upon the blood of the slain.

Simon observed, with a degree of relief, that the beings could not pass through the smoke from the herbs and, by this time, the whole room was full of the pungent odour.

'Nothing can destroy us, mortal!' Ahriman-Cotys bellowed. 'Slay more – give me more! You may escape now – but I will sport with you both soon. The huntsmen of my servitor, Olympias, will hound you across the earth. You cannot escape. And when you are ours – you will both become the most willing of my slaves...'

Simon reached the doorway of the cavern, turned, bearing the insensible Camilla, and ran up the slippery tunnel.

Now he knew. Now he could no longer rationalize. He had seen too much.

Now he knew that reason had passed from the world and that the ancient gods had returned to rule once more.

CHAPTER FIVE

The body was strong enough. Ahriman had tested it to his satisfaction. He had given the vessel superhuman strength and vitality which it had used for what it thought were its own purposes.

Alexander, though he possessed little of his own personality now, was ready. Soon entire populations would be the slaves of Ahriman, their bodies bent to him. Darkness such as the world had never known would come. Ormuzd and the Forces of Light would be vanquished for ever.

Ahriman had many facets – many names. Shaitan was another.

Now Alexander's captains gathered. They were loyal to him, would do his bidding – would become Ahriman's agents in bringing Hell to the surface of the Earth.

323 BC. A time of omens of evil. A turning point in history.

Alexander rose from his bed. He walked like an automaton and called for his slaves. They washed him, dressed him, and clad him in his golden armour.

'Hail, Jupiter-Ammon!' they intoned as he strode from the room and walked steadily to the chamber where his generals and advisors awaited him.

Ptolemy stood up as Alexander entered. His master seemed no different, yet there was a strange, detached air about him.

'Greetings, Jupiter-Ammon,' he said bowing low. Normally he refused to designate Alexander by the name of the God – but this time he was wary, remembering perhaps how Alexander had killed his close friend Clitus in Bactria.

Anaxarchus also bowed. The remaining ten did the same.

Alexander seated himself in the middle of the long table. The leather joints of the golden armour groaned as he bent. There was food and maps on the table. He stuffed a bit of bread into his mouth and unrolled a map, chewing. The twelve men waited nervously for him to speak.

Studying the map, Alexander held out his goblet. Ptolemy filled it with wine from a long-necked bottle of brass. Alexander drank it in a single gulp. Ptolemy replenished the cup.

Simon and Camilla had fled from Pela. The night was like a clammy cloak about them and lightning split the sky, rain hurling itself like tiny spears against their faces.

Camilla rode slightly behind Simon, following him in a terror-filled flight towards the East.

There was no other direction they might go and Simon needed to find Abaris the Magi and get his help, though Alexander still dwelled in Babylon.

Behind them now they heard the Huntsmen of Olympias – great dogs baying, horns sounding, and wild shouts urging the hounds on. And these huntsmen were not mortal – but loaned to Olympias by Ahriman that they both might sport with the fleeing humans.

They caught glimpses of their pursuers – things of legend. Offspring of Cerberus, the three-headed dog which guarded the gates of Hades – dogs with the tails of serpents and with snakes twining round their necks; great, flat, hideous-eyed heads, and huge teeth.

The huntsmen rode on the progeny of Pegasus, winged horses which skimmed over the ground, white and beautiful, fast as the North Wind.

And on the backs of the horses – the huntsmen. The grinning shades of dead villains, spewed from Hades to do Ahriman's work. Beside them loped the leopard-women, the Maenades, worshippers of Bacchus.

Behind all these came a screaming multitude of ghouls, demons and were-beasts, released from the depths of Hell.

For two weeks they had been thus pursued and Simon and Camilla were well aware that they could have been caught many times. Ahriman – as he had threatened – was sporting with them.

But still they pushed their horses onwards until they had reached the Bosphorus, hired a boat, and were on the open sea.

Then came the new phantoms to haunt them. Sea-shapes, rearing reptilian monsters, things with blazing eyes which swam just beneath the surface and occasionally put clawed hands on the sides of the boat.

Simon realized at last that all this was calculated to torment them and drive them mad, to give in to Ahriman's evil will.

Camilla, Simon could see, was already beginning to weaken. But he kept tight hold of sanity – and his purpose. Whether the Fates wished it or not, he knew what he must do, had taken upon himself a mission. He refused to attend to anything but that – and his strength aided Camilla.

Soon, Simon knew, the Evil One would realize that he could not break his spirit – then they would be doomed for Ahriman had the power to snuff them out. He prayed to Ormuzd, in whom he now believed with a fervour stemming from his deep need of something to which he could cling, and prayed that he might have a little more time – time to get to Babylon and do what he had taken upon himself to do.

Over the barren plains of Asia Minor they rode and all the nights of their journey the wild huntsmen screamed in their wake until Simon at least could turn sometimes and laugh at them, taunting them with words which were half-mad ravings.

He had little time, he knew.

One night, while great clouds loomed across the sky, they lost their way.

Simon had planned to follow the Euphrates on the banks of which was built Babylon, but in the confusion of the shrieking night he lost his way and it was not until the following morning that they sighted a river.

With relief, they rode towards it. The days were theirs – no phantoms came to torment them in the sunlight. Soon, Simon knew with a feeling of elation, they would be in Babylon with

Abaris and the Magi to aid them against the hordes of Ahriman.

All day they rode, keeping to the cracked bed of the river, dried in the heat of the searing sun. When dusk came, Simon calculated, they should reach the outskirts of Babylon. Which was well, for their horses were by now gaunt skeletons, plodding and tripping in the river bed, and Camilla was swaying, pale and fainting, in the saddle.

The sun began to go down lividly on the horizon as they urged the weary horses forward and already in their ears they heard the faint howling of the Maenades, the insane howlings of Cerberus's spawn. The nightmare of the nights was soon to begin again.

'Pray to Ormuzd that we reach the city in time,' Simon said wearily.

'Another such night and I fear my sanity will give way,' Camilla replied.

The howling, insensate cries of the Bacchae grew louder, in their ears and, turning in the saddle, Simon saw behind him the dim shapes of their pursuers – shapes which grew stronger with the deepening darkness.

They turned the bend in the river and the shape of a city loomed ahead.

But then, as they drew closer, Simon's heart fell.

This desolate, jagged ruin, this vast and deserted place was not Babylon! This city was dead – a place where a man, also, might die.

Now the armies of Alexander gathered. And they gathered, unbeknownst to them, not for material conquest but for a greater conquest – to destroy the power of Light and ensure the powers of Darkness of lasting rule.

Great armies gathered, all metal and leather and disciplined flesh.

323 BC and a sick man, drawing vitality from a supernatural source – a man possessed – ruled the known world, ordered its fighting men, controlled its inhabitants.

Alexander of Macedonia. Alexander the Great. Son of Zeus, Jupiter-Ammon. He had united the world under a single monarch – himself. And, united, it would fall . . .

In Babylon, oldest city of the ancient world, Alexander gave his orders to his captains. One hundred and forty-four miles square was Babylon, flanking each side of the great River

Euphrates, embanked with walls of brick, closed by gates of bronze. Dominating the city was the Temple of Baal, rising upwards and consisting of eight storeys gradually diminishing in width, ascended by a flight of steps winding around the whole building on the outside. Standing on its topmost tower, Alexander surveyed the mighty city which he had chosen as the base for his military operations. From here he could see the fabulous hanging gardens built by Nebuchadnezzar, laid out upon terraces which were raised one above the other on arches. The streets of the city were straight, intersecting one another at right angles.

Babylon, which had brooded for centuries, producing scientists, scholars, artists, great kings, and great priests, splendid warriors, and powerful conquerors. Babylon, whose rulers, the Chaldaeans, worshipped the heavenly bodies and let them guide their law-making.

Babylon, city of secrets and enlightenment. Babylon, soon to be abased by the most terrible blight of evil the world had known. The forces of light were scattered, broken by Alexander's conquerings, and Alexander himself had become the focus for the forces of evil. Soon the world would sink into darkness.

Desperately the adherents of Light strove to find a way to stop him, but they were weakened, outlawed. Little pockets of them, chief of these being the Magi of Persia, strove to stand against him – but it was almost futile. Slowly, surely, implacably, evil Ahriman and his minions were gaining ascendancy.

And Simon of Byzantium had failed to reach Babylon and contact the Magi.

Simon and Camilla had never seen such a vast city. The crumbling walls encompassed a fantastic area ... Where they were still intact three chariots might have passed each other on them and they were over 100 feet high. Broken towers rose everywhere, hundreds of them, twice as high as the walls.

But the wind moaned in the towers and great owls with wide, terrible eyes hooted and glided about them, seeming the city's only occupants.

Camilla reached over and found Simon's hand. He gripped it to give her a comfort he did not himself feel.

Behind them they still heard the hunters. Wearied, they could go no further and their tired brains told them that here, among ruins, they would find no hiding place.

The slow clopping of their horses' hooves echoed in the empty city as they followed a broad, overgrown avenue through jagged shadows thrown by the broken buildings. Now Simon could see that the city had been destroyed by fire. But it was cold, chillingly cold in the light of the huge moon which hung overhead like an omen of despair.

The cries of the huntsmen joined the hoots of the owls, a horrid cacophony of fearful, foreboding sound.

But now they could no longer run before their hunters. Fatalistically they must wait – to be caught.

Then suddenly, ahead of them. Simon saw a dark shape framed against the moonlight. He drew his sword and halted his horse. He was too tired to attack, waited for the figure to approach.

When it came closer it flung back the cowl of its cloak and Simon gasped in relief and astonishment.

'Abaris! I was going to seek you in Babylon. What are you doing here?'

'Waiting for you, Simon.' The priest smiled gently and sympathetically. He, also, looked dreadfully worn. His long un-Persian face was pale and there were lines about his mouth.

'Waiting for me? How could you have known that I should lose my way and come here?'

'It was ordained by the Fates that you should do so. Do not question that.'

'Where are we?'

'In the ruins of forgotten Nineveh. This was a great city once, larger than Babylon and almost as powerful. The Medes and Babylonians razed it 300 years ago.'

'Nineveh,' Camilla breathed, 'there are legends about it.'

'Forget those you have heard and remember this – you are safe here, but not for long. The remnants of Ormuzd's supporters fled here and form a strong company – but not so strong that we can last for ever against Ahriman's dreadful minions.'

'Now I realize what happened,' Simon said. 'We followed the Tigris river instead of the Euphrates.'

'That is so.'

Behind them the wild baying came closer. Abaris signed to them to follow him.

Abaris led them into a dark sidestreet and then into a maze of alleys choked with fallen masonry, weed-grown and dank. By a small two-storied house which was still virtually intact, he stopped, withdrew a bolt and motioned them inside. They took their horses with them.

The house was much larger inside than it seemed and Simon guessed that it consisted of several houses now. There were about two hundred people in the large room behind the one they had entered. They sat, squatted, and stood in positions of acute weariness. Many were priests. Simon recognized several cults.

Here were Chaldaeans, the ruling caste of Babylon, proud and arrogant seeming still, Egyptian priests of Osiris, a Hebrew rabbi. Others Simon did not recognize and Abaris whispered answers to his questions. There were Brahmin from India, Pythagoreans from Samos and Crotona in Etrusca, Parsees from the deserts of Kerman and Hindustan, Druids from the far North, from the bleak islands on the world's edge, blind priests of the Cimmerians who, history told, were the ancestors of the Thracians and Macedonians.

Alexander had destroyed their temples, scattered them. Only in the far North and the far East were the priests of Light still organized and they had sent deputations to Nineveh to aid their brothers.

And Alexander's wrath had been mainly turned on the Zoroastrians, the Persian and Chaldaean Magi, strongest of the sects who worshipped the powers of Law and Light.

Here they all were, weary men, tired by a battle which required no material weapons yet sapped their vitality as they strove to hold Ahriman at bay.

Abaris introduced Simon and Camilla to the gathering, and he appeared to know the best part of their story, how they had been present at the Cottyttia, how they had fled from Pela, hounded by the infernal hordes, crossed the Bosphorus and came, at length, to fallen Nineveh.

Outside, Nineveh's streets were filled with a hideous throng, weird beasts of all kinds, dead souls, and malevolent denizens of Hell. Three-headed, snake-tailed dogs, winged horses, chimerae, basilisks, sphinx, centaurs and griffins, fire-spewing salamanders. All roamed the broken streets hunting for Ahriman's prey. But there was an area where they could not pass – an area which gave out emanations which meant death for them, so they avoided this area.

For the meantime, Simon and Camilla were safe. But it was stalemate, for while they were in Nineveh, secure against the forces of evil, Alexander strode the golden towers of Babylon and readied the world for the final conquest.

CHAPTER SIX

Abaris told Simon: 'Alexander slew your friend Hano, the Phoenician a week ago.'

Simon cursed: 'May the Harpies pluck his eyes from his skull!'

Camilla said: 'Do not evoke the Harpies, also. We have enough to contend with.'

Abaris half smiled, waved his hand towards a small table in a corner of the room. 'You had better eat now. You must be very tired.'

Gratefully the pair began to eat, drinking the spiced wine of the Magi – a wine which was unnaturally invigorating. Abaris said, while they ate:

'Ahriman dwells constantly, now, in Alexander's body. He intends to make a final campaign, north and east, to subdue the barbarian tribes of Gaul and the Dark Island, crush the Indian kings, and rule the entire world. And, it seems, he will be able to do all this through his vessel, Alexander – for the whole world already responds to Alexander's whims; he commands the fighting men and a host of subject kings and princes. It will be an easy matter ...'

'But he must be stopped,' Simon said. 'Have you no means of stopping him?'

'For months we have tried to fight the forces of evil, without success. We have almost given up and wait for the coming of Darkness.'

'I believe I know what can be done,' Simon said, 'and it will be a cleaner method than that used by any of you. With your aid I must get to Babylon – and with your aid I will do what I must.'

'Very well, my friend,' Abaris said, 'tell me what you need.'

Kettle-drums beat and brazen trumpets sounded. The dust

swelled into the heated air before the feet of Alexander's armies. Coarse soldiers' voices bellowed orders and the captains rode in military pomp at the head of their armies. Plumes of dyed horse-hair bobbed bright beneath the sun, horses stamped, bedecked in trappings of blue and red and yellow, bronze armour glinted like gold and shields clashed against javelins, lances rose like wheat above the heads of the marching men, their tips bright and shining.

Hard-faced warriors moved in ordered ranks – men from Macedonia, Thrace, Greece, Bactria, Babylon, Persia, Assyria, Arabia, Egypt, and the Hebrew nations.

Millions of fighting men. Millions of souls trained for slaying and destruction.

And ordering them, one man – Alexander the Great. Alexander in his hawk-like helm of gold, standing on the steps of the Temple of Baal in Babylon and readying his hosts for the final conquest. Alexander in the trappings of a Persian monarch, absolute ruler of the civilized world. In his right hand a gleaming sword, in his left the sceptre of the law giver. In his body, possessing it, flowing through it, dominating it – black evil. Ahriman, Master of Darkness, soon to commit the absolute crime – the destruction of Law, the birth of the Dark Millenium.

Around Babylon, mighty armies were camped and it was easy for Simon to enter the city, for many mercenaries had flocked to fight beneath Alexander's banner.

Wrapped around the Thracian was what seemed to be a simple stained black soldier's cloak, but inside, lining it, was richer stuff marked with curious symbols, the Cloak of the Magi, it served to ward off evil and kept Simon, for the time being, safe from Ahriman's attentions.

That day he stood in the square surrounding the Temple of Baal and heard Ahriman speak through Alexander. It was dangerous for him to do this, he knew, but he had to see the man again.

Alexander addressed the populace.

'People of Babylon, my warriors, the morrow sees the start of our final conquests. Soon no spot of soil, no drop of ocean shall be independent of our Empire, I, Jupiter-Ammon, have come to Earth to cleanse it of heretics, to destroy unbelievers and bring the new age to the world. Those who murmur against me shall die. Those who oppose me shall suffer torments and will wish to die. Those who would halt my plans –

they shall never die but will be sent living to Hades. Now the armies are marshalled. Already we control most of the world, save for a few patches to the North and a few to the East. Within months these, also, will be ours. Worship us, my people, for Zeus has returned from Olympus, born of a woman named Olympias, father of the son, son and father are One. We are Jupiter-Ammon and our will is divine!'

The people screamed their exultation at these words and bowed low before the man-god who stood so proud above them.

Only Simon remained standing, clad in his bagged and dusty cloak, his face thin, and his eyes bright. He stared up at Alexander who saw him almost immediately, opened his mouth to order the unbeliever destroyed, and then closed it again.

For long moments the two men stared into one another's eyes – the one representing total evil, the other representing the forces of Light. In that great, hushed city nothing seemed to stir and the air carried only faint sounds of military preparation from behind the city walls.

There was a peculiar communication between them. Simon felt as if he were looking into the Abyss of Hell and yet sensed something else lurking in the eyes – something cleaner that had long since been subdued and almost erased.

Then he was in motion, running for the steps that wound upwards around the Temple of Baal.

He bounded up the steps, twenty, fifty, a hundred and he had still not reached Alexander who stood like a statue awaiting him.

The God-Emperor turned as Simon finally reached the upper level. As if Simon were not there he strode back through the shaded pillars and into the building. That was where Simon confronted him.

Sunlight lanced through the pillars and criss-crossed the place in a network of shadow and light. Alexander now sat on a huge golden throne, his chin resting in one hand, his back bent as if in meditation. Steps led up to the dais on which the throne was placed. Simon stopped at the first step and looked up at the conqueror of the world.

Alexander leaned back in his throne and clasped his hands in front of him. He smiled slowly, at first a smile of irony which twisted into a grin of malice and hatred.

'There is a sacred bull in Memphis,' Alexander said slowly, 'which is called Apis. It is an oracle. Seven years ago I went to Memphis to hear the sacred bull and to ascertain whether it had, indeed, oracular powers. When it saw me it spoke a rhyme. I have remembered that rhyme for seven years.'

Simon drew the Cloak of the Magi closer about him. 'What did it say?' he asked in a strained half-whisper.

Alexander shook his head. 'I did not understand it until recently. It went:

The City that thy father lost shall fall to thee,
The City that gives birth to fools shall bear a sword.
The City that thy father lost shall be its home.
The City that thou mak'st thy home shall feel its edge.'

Simon brooded over this for a moment and then he nodded, understanding.

'Byzantium, Abdera, Byzantium – Babylon,' he said.

'How sharp is the sword?' Alexander asked and changed shape.

A dazzling orange-golden haze burst upwards and a black and scarlet figure stood framed in the centre. It vaguely resembled Alexander but was twice as high, twice as broad, and bore a weirdly wrought staff in its hand.

'So!' Simon cried, 'At last you show your true shape. You bear the Wand of Ahriman, I see!'

'Aye, mortal – and that only Ahriman may bear.'

From beneath the Cloak of the Magi, Simon produced a short javelin and a small shield of about ten inches in diameter. He held the shield in front of his face and through it could see unnerving and alien shapes where the figure of Ahriman stood. He was seeing the true shape of Ahriman, not the warped and metamorphosed body of Alexander.

He drew back his arm and hurled the javelin at a certain spot in the intricate supernatural pattern.

There came an unearthly groaning and muttering from the figure. It threw up its arms and the wand flickered and sent a bolt of black lightning at Simon who put up his shield again and repelled it, though he was hurled back against a far column. He leaped to his feet, drawing his sword and saw that, as Abaris had told him, Alexander had resumed his usual shape.

The God-King staggered and frowned. He turned and saw Simon standing there, sword in hand.

'What's this?' he said.

'Prepare to fight me, Alexander!' Simon cried.

'But why?'

'You must never know why.'

And Simon leaped forward.

Alexander drew his own lovely blade, a slim thing of strong tempering, of glowing-star-metal with a handle of black onyx.

The iron clashed with a musical note, so fine were both blades and the two men feinted, parried, and stabbed, fighting in the Greek manner, using the points of their swords rather than the edges.

Alexander came in swiftly, grasped Simon's wrist and pushed his sword back, bringing his own sword in, but Simon sidestepped just in time, and the blade grazed his thigh. Alexander cursed a very human curse and grinned briefly at Simon in the old, earlier manner.

'You are swift, my friend.'

Simon disliked this. It was harder to fight such a light-hearted and likeable warrior than the thing which Alexander had earlier been. It was almost unjust – yet the action had to be made.

In and out of the network of light and shadow the two men danced, skipping away, coming in close, swords flashing, and the music of their meeting echoing about the Temple of Baal.

Then Alexander's soldiers came running into the place but Alexander cried:

'Stand back – I do not know why this man attacked me, but I have never fought such a swordsman before and would not miss the privilege. If he wins – free him.'

Bewildered, the guards retreated.

For hours the fight continued, each man evenly matched. Dusk came, sunset flooding the Temple with blood-red rays. Like two archetypal gods they fought on, thrusting, parrying, employing every tactic at their command.

Then Alexander, whose earlier sickness had wearied him, stumbled and Simon saw his opportunity, paused, deliberating the act, then rushed upon his opponent and struck him a terrible thrust in the lung.

'Go – be Charon's guest!' he cried.

Alexander went hurtling back to land with a crash, sprawled

on the steps of the dais. Again the watching warriors rushed forward, but Alexander waved them back.

'Do not tell the people how I met my end,' he gasped. 'I have united the world – let it stay united in the confidence that a – a – god created that unity. Perhaps that will serve to ensure peace . . .'

Dismissed, the guards returned, wondering, down the steps of the Temple and Simon and the dying Alexander were left alone in the half-light while a wind blew up and sent a cold chill through the silent columns.

'I remember you now,' Alexander said, blood beginning to trickle from his mouth. 'You are the Thracian. What happened – I remember interviewing you and then the rest is hazed in blackness and chaos – what happened then?'

Simon shook his head.

'Call it madness,' he said. 'A madness, which came upon you.'

In the shadows behind the throne he saw a black mist begin to form. Hurriedly he shouted: 'Abaris – quickly!'

The priest appeared then. He had slipped up the steps and had been standing behind a column. Others followed him. He motioned them in. They began a weird and beautiful chanting, advancing towards the hazy form behind the throne, making peculiar passes in the air.

After them, Camilla appeared and stood framed in a gap between two columns, the wind ruffling her hair.

Alexander grasped Simon's arm. 'I remember a prophesy – one made by the Oracle of Memphis. How did it go?'

Simon quoted it.

'Yes,' Alexander gasped. 'So you are the sword which the City of Fools, Abdera, bore . . .'

'What shall we remember of you, Alexander?' Simon asked quietly as there came a commotion behind the throne which was now surrounded by chanting Magi. He looked up. The priests seemed to be straining to hold back some horrible force which whimpered and moaned at them, yet was still very strong.

'Remember? Will not the world always remember me? My dream was to unite the world and bring peace. But a nightmare interrupted that dream, I think . . .'

'Your father's dream and yours,' Simon said.

'My father – I hated him – yet he was a good and wise king,

and moulded me for a purpose. Aristotle was my teacher, you know. But I had other indoctrination. My mother Olympias, taught me peculiar things which I cannot remember now.'

'Let us hope no one shall ever know them again,' Simon breathed.

'What has happened?' Alexander asked again. Then his eyes closed. 'What did I do?'

'You did nothing that was not for the good of the world,' Simon told him. Alexander was dead. 'But,' the Thracian added quietly as the Emperor's grip loosened and the limp hand fell to the marble of the step, 'that which possessed you wrought harm. You could not help it. You were born to perish...'

He rose and called: 'Abaris. Abaris – he is dead.'

The chanting ceased. The black shape still hovered there, veins of orange-gold, black, and scarlet throbbing in it like blood-vessels. Simon and the priests fell back.

The shape shot towards Alexander's corpse, sank down over it. The corpse jerked but then was still again. For an instant a face – the face Simon had seen at the Rites of Cotys in Pela – appeared.

'There will be others, never fear!' Ahriman said and vanished.

Abaris went over to Alexander's corpse and made a pass over the wound. When Simon looked there was no sign of a wound.

'We'll say he died of a fever,' Abaris said softly. 'It was well known that he was ill. They will believe us – we will let the Chaldaeans speak in Babylon for they long ruled the people before Alexander's coming.'

Simon said: 'I knew that clean steel could end this matter for us.'

Abaris looked at him a trifle cynically.

'Without our magic to drive Ahriman out of Alexander's body for the time you needed, you would never have succeeded.'

'That's true, I suppose.'

Abaris continued:

'That was the solution. Ahriman works through many people – but he needs a single human vessel if he is to carry out his Great Plan. Several have been born in the past – others will be born again. Fanatical conquerors who will set out to rule the world. Men with superhuman vitality, the power of dominating great masses of people and driving them to do that one man's will. Yes, Ahriman – under whatever name he takes – will try again. That is certain.'

'Meanwhile,' Simon said as Camilla came up to him, 'we have succeeded in halting Ahriman this time.'

'Who knows?' Abaris said. 'History will show if we were in time or not.'

Simon said gravely: 'I am not sure what Alexander, himself, was. He could have been a force for good or evil. He was something of both. But the evil gained ascendency towards the end. Was I right to kill him? Could not his course have been turned so that the good in him could have continued his plan to unite the world in peace?'

'That may have been possible,' the priest said thoughtfully, 'but we men set limits to our endeavours – it is easier that way. Perhaps, in time, we will not stop short but will learn to choose the harder paths and so achieve more positive results. As it is we strive merely to keep a balance. One day Alexander's dream may be realized and the world united. Let us hope that the unity will be inspired by Ormuzd. Then it may be possible to build.'

Simon sighed and made his body relax.

'Meanwhile, as you say, we'll strive for balance alone. Pray to Ormuzd, priest and pray that men will one day cease to need their gods.'

'That day may come and, if I am right, the gods themselves will welcome it.'

Abaris bowed and left Simon and Camilla staring at one another. For a long time they remained so before embracing.

BEHOLD THE MAN

He has no material power as the god-emperors had; he has only a following of desert people and fishermen. They tell him he is a god; he believes them. The followers of Alexander said: 'He is unconquerable, therefore he is a god.' The followers of this man do not think at all; he was their act of spontaneous creation. Now he leads them, this Nazarene madman called Jesus of Nazareth.

And he spoke, saying unto them: Yeah verily I was *Karl Glogauer and now I am Jesus the Messiah, the Christ.*

And it was so.

CHAPTER ONE

The time machine was a sphere full of milky fluid in which the traveller floated, enclosed in a rubber suit, breathing through a mask attached to a hose leading to the wall of the machine. The sphere cracked as it landed and the fluid spilled into the dust and was soaked up. Instinctively, Glogauer curled himself into a ball as the level of the liquid fell and he sank to the yielding plastic of the sphere's inner lining. The instruments, cryptographic, unconventional, were still and silent. The sphere shifted and rolled as the last of the liquid dripped from the great gash in its side.

Momentarily, Glogauer's eyes opened and closed, then his mouth stretched in a kind of yawn and his tongue fluttered and he uttered a groan that turned into an ululation.

He heard himself. The Voice of Tongues, he thought. The language of the unconscious. But he could not guess what he was saying.

His body became numb and he shivered. His passage through time had not been easy and even the thick fluid had not wholly protected him, though it had doubtless saved his life. Some ribs were certainly broken. Painfully, he straightened his arms and legs and began to crawl over the slippery plastic towards the crack in the machine. He could see harsh sunlight, a sky like shimmering steel. He pulled himself halfway through the crack, closing his eyes as the full strength of the sunlight struck them. He lost consciousness.

Christmas term, 1949. He was nine years old, born two years after his father had reached England from Austria.

The other children were screaming with laughter in the gravel of the playground. The game had begun earnestly enough and somewhat nervously Karl had joined in in the same spirit. Now he was crying.

'Let me *down*! Please, Mervyn, stop it!'

They had tied him with his arms spreadeagled against the wire-netting of the playground fence. It bulged outwards under his weight and one of the posts threatened to come loose. Mervyn Williams, the boy who had proposed the game, began to shake the post so that Karl was swung heavily back and forth on the netting.

'Stop it!'

He saw that his cries only encouraged them and he clenched his teeth, becoming silent.

He slumped, pretending unconsciousness; the school ties they had used as bonds cut into his wrists. He heard the children's voices drop.

'Is he all right?' Molly Turner was whispering.

'He's only kidding,' Williams replied uncertainly.

He felt them untying him, ther fingers fumbling with the knots. Deliberately, he sagged, then fell to his knees, grazing them on the gravel, and dropped face down to the ground.

Distantly, for he was half-convinced by his own deception, he heard their worried voices.

Williams shook him.

'Wake up, Karl. Stop mucking about.'

He stayed where he was, losing his sense of time until he heard Mr Matson's voice over the general babble.

'What on earth were you doing, Williams?'

'It was a play, sir, about Jesus. Karl was being Jesus. We tied him to the fence. It was his idea, sir. It was only a game, sir.'

Karl's body was stiff, but he managed to stay still, breathing shallowly.

'He's not a strong boy like you, Williams. You should have known better.'

'I'm sorry, sir. I'm really sorry.' Williams sounded as if he were crying.

Karl felt himself lifted; felt the triumph . . .

He was being carried along. His head and side were so painful that he felt sick. He had had no chance to discover where exactly the time machine had brought him, but, turning his head now, he could see by the way the man on his right was dressed that he was at least in the Middle East.

He had meant to land in the year AD 29 in the wilderness beyond Jerusalem, near Bethlehem. Were they taking him to Jerusalem now?

He was on a stretcher that was apparently made of animal skins; this indicated that he was probably in the past at any rate. Two men were carrying the stretcher on their shoulders. Others walked on both sides. There was a smell of sweat and animal fat and a musty smell he could not identify. They were walking towards a line of hills in the distance.

He winced as the stretcher lurched and the pain in his side increased. For the second time he passed out.

He woke up briefly, hearing voices. They were speaking what was evidently some form of Aramaic. It was night, perhaps, for it seemed very dark. They were no longer moving. There was straw beneath him. He was relieved. He slept.

> *In those days came John the Baptist preaching in the wilderness of Judaea. And saying, Repent ye: for the kingdom of heaven is at hand. For this is he that was spoken of by the prophet Esaias, saying, The voice of one crying in the wilderness. Prepare ye the way of the Lord, make his paths straight. And the same John had his raiment of camel's hair, and a leathern girdle about his loins; and his meat was locusts and wild honey. Then went out to him Jerusalem, and all Judaea, and all the region round about Jordan, And were baptized of him in Jordan, confessing their sins.*
>
> (Matthew 3 : 1–6)

They were washing him. He felt the cold water running over his naked body. They had managed to strip off his protective suit. There were now thick layers of cloth against his ribs on the right, and bands of leather bound them to him.

He felt very weak now, and hot, but there was less pain.

He was in a building – or perhaps a cave, it was too gloomy to tell – lying on a heap of straw that was saturated by the water. Above him, two men continued to sluice water down on him from their earthenware pots. They were stern-faced, heavily-bearded men, in cotton robes.

He wondered if he could form a sentence they might understand. His knowledge of written Aramaic was good, but he was not sure of certain pronounciations.

He cleared his throat. 'Where – be – this – place?'

They frowned, shaking their heads and lowering their water jars.

'I – seek – a – Nazarene – Jesus...'

'Nazarene. Jesus.' One of the men repeated the words, but they did not seem to mean anything to him. He shrugged.

The other, however, only repeated the word Nazarene, speaking it slowly as if it had some special significance for him. He muttered a few words to the other man and went towards the entrance of the room.

Karl Glogauer continued to try to say something the remaining man would understand.

'What – year – doth – the Roman Emperor – sit – Rome?'

It was a confusing question to ask, he realized. He knew Christ had been crucified in the fifteenth year of Tiberius's reign, and that was why he had asked the question. He tried to phrase it better.

'How many – year – doth Tiberius rule?'

'Tiberius?' The man frowned.

Glogauer's ear was adjusting to the accent now and he tried to simulate it better. 'Tiberius. The emperor of the Romans. How many years has he ruled?'

'How many?' The man shook his head. 'I know not.'

At least Glogauer had managed to make himself understood.

'Where is this place?' he asked.

'It is the wilderness beyond Machaerus,' the man replied. 'Know you not that?'

Machaerus lay to the south-east of Jerusalem, on the other side of the Dead Sea. There was no doubt that he was in the past and that the period was some time in the reign of Tiberius, for the man had recognized the name easily enough.

His companion was now returning, bringing with him a huge fellow with heavily muscled hairy arms and a great barrel chest. He carried a big staff in one hand. He was dressed in animal skins and was well over six feet tall. His black, curly hair was long, and he had a black, bushy beard that covered the upper half of his chest. He moved like an animal and his large, piercing brown eyes looked reflectively at Glogauer.

When he spoke, it was in a deep voice, but too rapidly for Glogauer to follow. It was Glogauer's turn to shake his head.

The big man squatted down beside him. 'Who art thou?'

Glogauer paused. He had not planned to be found in this way. He had intended to disguise himself as a traveller from Syria, hoping that the local accents would be different enough to explain his own unfamiliarity with the language. He decided that it was best to stick to this story and hope for the best.

'I am from the north,' he said.

'Not from Egypt?' the big man asked. It was as if he had expected Glogauer to be from there. Glogauer decided that if this was what the big man thought, he might just as well agree to it.

'I came out of Egypt two years since,' he said.

The big man nodded, apparently satisfied. 'So you are a magus from Egypt. That is what we thought. And your name is Jesus, and you are the Nazarene.'

'I *seek* Jesus, the Nazarene,' Glogauer said.

'Then what is your name?' The man seemed disappointed.

Glogauer could not give his own name. It would sound too strange to them. On impulse, he gave his father's first name. 'Emmanuel,' he said.

The man nodded, again satisfied. 'Emmanuel.'

Glogauer realized belatedly that the choice of name had been an unfortunate one in the circumstances, for Emmanuel meant in Hebrew 'God with us' and doubtless had a mystic significance for his questioner.

'And what is your name?' he asked.

The man straightened up, looking broodingly down on Glogauer. 'You do not know me? You have not heard of John, called the Baptist?'

Glogauer tried to hide his surprise, but evidently John the Baptist saw that his name was familiar. He nodded his shaggy head. 'You do know me, I see. Well, magus, now I must decide, eh?'

'What must you decide?' Glogauer asked nervously.

'If you be the friend of the prophecies or the false one we have been warned against by Adonai. The Romans would deliver me into the hands of mine enemies, the children of Herod.'

'Why is that?'

'You must know why, for I speak against the Romans who enslave Judaea, and I speak against the unlawful things that Herod does, and I prophesy the time when all those who are not righteous shall be destroyed and Adonai's kingdom will be restored on Earth as the old prophets said it would be. I say to the people "Be ready for that day when ye shall take up the sword to do Adonai's will". The unrighteous know that they will perish on this day, and they would destroy me.'

Despite the intensity of his words, John's tone was matter of fact. There was no hint of insanity or fanaticism in his face or bearing. He sounded most of all like an Anglican vicar reading a sermon whose meaning for him had lost its edge.

The essence of what he said, Karl Glogauer realized, was that he was arousing the people to throw out the Romans and their puppet Herod and establish a more 'righteous' regime. The attributing of this plan to 'Adonai' (one of the spoken names of Jahweh and meaning The Lord) seemed, as many scholars had guessed in the twentieth century, a means of giving the plan extra weight. In a world where politics and religion, even in the west, were inextricably bound together, it was necessary to ascribe a supernatural origin to the plan.

Indeed, Glogauer thought, it was more than likely that John believed his idea had been inspired by God, for the Greeks on the other side of the Mediterranean had not yet stopped arguing about the origins of inspiration – whether it originated in a man's head or was placed there by the gods. That John accepted him as an Egyptian magician of some kind did not surprise Glogauer particularly, either. The circumstances of his arrival must have seemed extaordinarily miraculous and at the same time acceptable, particularly to a sect like the Essenes who practised self-mortification and starvation and must be quite used to seeing visions in this hot wilderness. There was no doubt now that these people were the neurotic Essenes, whose ritual washing – baptism – and self-deprivation, coupled with the almost paranoiac mysticism that led them to invent secret languages and the like, was a sure indication of their mentally unbalanced condition. All this occurred to Glogauer, the psychiatrist manqué, but Glogauer the man was torn between the poles of extreme rationalism and the desire to be convinced by the mysticism itself.

'I must meditate,' John said, turning towards the cave entrance. 'I must pray. You will remain here until guidance is sent to me.'

He left the cave, striding rapidly away.

Glogauer sank back on the wet straw. He was without doubt in a limestone cave, and the atmosphere in the cave was surprisingly humid. It must be very hot outside. He felt drowsy.

CHAPTER TWO

Five years in the past. Nearly two thousand in the future. Lying in the hot, sweaty bed with Monica. Once again, another attempt to make normal love had metamorphosed into the performance of minor aberrations which seemed to satisfy her better than anything else.

Their real courtship and fulfilment was yet to come. As usual, it would be verbal. As usual it would find its climax in argumentative anger.

'I suppose you're going to tell me you're not satisfied again.' She accepted the lighted cigarette he handed to her in the darkness.

'I'm all right,' he said.

There was silence for a while as they smoked.

Eventually, and in spite of knowing what the result would be if he did so, he found himself talking.

'It's ironic, isn't it?' he began.

He waited for her reply. She would delay for a little while yet.

'What is?' she said at last.

'All this. You spend all day trying to help sexual neurotics to become normal. You spend your nights doing what they do.'

'Not to the same extent. You know it's all a matter of degree.'

'So you say.'

He turned his head and looked at her face in the starlight from the window. She was a gaunt-featured redhead, with the calm, professional seducer's voice of the psychiatric social worker that she was. It was a voice that was soft, reasonable, and insincere. Only occasionally, when she became particularly agitated did her voice begin to indicate her real character. Her features never seemed to be in repose, even when she slept. Her eyes were forever wary, her movements rarely spontaneous. Every inch of her was protected, which was probably why she got so little pleasure from ordinary lovemaking.

'You just can't let yourself go, can you?' he said.

'Oh, shut up, Karl. Have a look at yourself if you're looking for a neurotic mess.'

Both were amateur psychiatrists – she a psychiatric social worker, he merely a reader, a dabbler, though he had done a year's study some time ago when he had planned to become a psychiatrist. They used the terminology of psychiatry freely. They felt happier if they could name something.

He rolled away from her, groping for the ashtray on the bedside table, catching a glance of himself in the dressing table mirror. He was a sallow, intense, moody Jewish bookseller, with a head full of images and unresolved obsessions, a body full of emotions. He always lost these arguments with Monica. Verbally, she was the dominant one. This kind of exchange often seemed to him more perverse than their love-making, where usually at least his role was masculine. Essentially, he realized, he was passive, masochistic, indecisive. Even his anger, which came frequently, was impotent. Monica was ten years older than he was, ten years more bitter. As an individual, of course, she had far more dynamism than he had; but as a psychiatric social worker she had had just as many failures. She plugged on, becoming increasingly cynical on the surface but still, perhaps, hoping for a few spectacular successes with patients. They tried to do too much, that was the trouble, he thought. The priests in the confessional supplied a panacea; the psychiatrists tried to cure, and most of the time they failed. But at least they tried, he thought, and then wondered if that was, after all, a virtue.

'I did look at myself,' he said.

Was she sleeping? He turned. Her wary eyes were still open, looking out of the window.

'I did look at myself,' he repeated. 'The way Jung did. "How can I help these persons if I am myself a fugitive and perhaps also suffer from the *morbus sacer* of a neurosis?" That's what Jung asked himself . . .'

'That old sensationalist. That old rationalizer of his own mysticism. No wonder you never became a psychiatrist.'

'I wouldn't have been any good. It was nothing to do with Jung . . .'

'Don't take it out on me . . .'

'You've told me yourself that you feel the same – you think it's useless . . .'

'After a hard week's work, I might say that. Give me another fag.'

He opened the packet on the bedside table and put two cigarettes in his mouth, lighting them and handing one to her.

Almost abstractedly, he noticed that the tension was increasing. The argument was, as ever, pointless. But it was not the argument that was the important thing; it was simply the expression of their essential relationship. He wondered if that were in any way important, either.

'You're not telling the truth.' He realized that there was no stopping now that the ritual was in full swing.

'I'm telling the practical truth. I've no compulsion to give up my work. I've no wish to be a failure . . .'

'Failure? You're more melodramatic than I am.'

'You're too earnest, Karl. You want to get out of yourself a bit.'

He sneered. 'If I were you, I'd give up my work, Monica. You're no more suited for it than I was.'

She shrugged. 'You're a petty bastard.'

'I'm not jealous of you, if that's what you think. You'd never understand what I'm looking for.'

Her laugh was artificial, brittle. 'Modern man in search of a soul, eh? Modern man in search of a crutch, I'd say. And you can take that any way you like.'

'We're destroying the myths that make the world go round.'

'Now you say "And what are we putting in their place?" You're stale and stupid, Karl. You've never looked rationally at anything – including yourself.'

'What of it. You say the myth is unimportant.'

'The reality that creates it is important.'

'Jung knew that the myth can also create the reality.'

'Which shows what a muddled old fool he was.'

He stretched his legs. In doing so, he touched hers and he recoiled. He scratched his head. She still lay there smoking, but she was smiling now.

'Come on,' she said. 'Let's have some stuff about Christ.'

He said nothing. She handed him the stub of her cigarette and he put it in the ashtray. He looked at his watch. It was two o'clock in the morning.

'Why do we do it?' he said.

'Because we must.' She put her hand to the back of his head and pulled it towards her breast. 'What else can we do?'

We Protestants must sooner or later face this question: Are we to understand the 'imitation of Christ' in the sense that we should copy his life and, if I may use the expression, ape his stigmata; or in the deeper sense that we are to live our own proper lives as truly as he lived his in all its implications? It is no easy matter to live a life that is modelled on Christ's, but it is unspeakably harder to live one's own life as truly as Christ lived his. Anyone who did this would ... be misjudged, derided, tortured and crucified ... A neurosis is a dissociation of personality.

(*Jung: Modern Man in Search of a Soul*)

For a month, John the Baptist was away and Glogauer lived with the Essenes, finding it surprisingly easy, as his ribs mended, to join in their daily life. The Essenes' township consisted of a mixture of single-storey houses, built of limestone and clay brick, and the caves that were to be found on both sides of the shallow valley. The Essenes shared their goods in common and this particular sect had wives, though many Essenes led completely monastic lives. The Essenes were also pacifists, refusing to own or to make weapons – yet this sect plainly tolerated the warlike Baptist. Perhaps their hatred of the Romans overcame their principles. Perhaps they were not sure of John's entire intention. Whatever the reason for their toleration, there was little doubt that John the Baptist was virtually their leader.

The life of the Essenes consisted of ritual bathing three times a day, of prayer and of work. The work was not difficult. Sometimes Glogauer guided a plough pulled by two other members of the sect, sometimes he looked after the goats that were allowed to graze on the hillsides. It was a peaceful, ordered life, and even the unhealthy aspects were so much a matter of routine that Glogauer hardly noticed them for anything else after a while.

Tending the goats, he would lie on a hill-top, looking out over the wilderness which was not a desert, but rocky scrubland sufficient to feed animals like goats or sheep. The scrubland was broken by low-lying bushes and a few small trees growing along the banks of the river that doubtless ran into the Dead Sea. It was uneven ground. In outline, it had the appearance of a stormy lake, frozen and turned yellow and brown. Beyond the Dead Sea lay Jerusalem. Obviously Christ had not entered the city for the last time yet. John the Baptist would have to die before that happened.

The Essenes' way of life was comfortable enough, for all its simplicity. They had given him a goatskin loin-cloth and a staff and, except for the fact that he was watched by day and night, he appeared to be accepted as a kind of lay member of the sect.

Sometimes they questioned him casually about his chariot – the time machine they intended soon to bring in from the desert – and he told them that it had borne him from Egypt to Syria and then to here. They accepted the miracle calmly. As he had suspected, they were used to miracles.

The Essenes had seen stranger things than his time machine. They had seen men walk on water and angels descend to and from heaven; they had heard the voice of God and His archangels as well as the tempting voice of Satan and his minions. They wrote all these things down in their vellum scrolls. They were merely a record of the supernatural as their other scrolls were records of their daily lives and of the news that travelling members of their sect brought to them.

They lived constantly in the presence of God and spoke to God and were answered by God when they had sufficiently mortified their flesh and starved themselves and chanted their prayers beneath the blazing sun of Judaea.

Karl Glogauer grew his hair long and let his beard come unchecked. He mortified his flesh and starved himself and chanted his prayers beneath the sun, as they did. But he rarely heard God and only once thought he saw an archangel with wings of fire.

In spite of his willingness to experience the Essenes' hallucinations, Glogauer was disappointed, but he was surprised that he felt so well considering all the self-inflicted hardships he had to undergo, and he also felt relaxed in the company of these men and women who were undoubtedly insane. Perhaps it was because their insanity was not so very different from his own that after a while he stopped wondering about it.

John the Baptist returned one evening, striding over the hills followed by twenty or so of his closest disciples. Glogauer saw him as he prepared to drive the goats into their cave for the night. He waited for John to get closer.

The Baptist's face was grim, but his expression softened as he saw Glogauer. He smiled and grasped him by the upper arm in the Roman fashion.

'Well, Emmanuel, you are our friend, as I thought you were.

Sent by Adonai to help us accomplish His will. You shall baptize me on the morrow, to show all the people that He is with us.'

Glogauer was tired. He had eaten very little and had spent most of the day in the sun, tending the goats. He yawned, finding it hard to reply. However, he was relieved. John had plainly been in Jerusalem trying to discover if the Romans had sent him as a spy. John now seemed reassured and trusted him.

He was worried, however, by the Baptist's faith in his powers.

'John,' he began. 'I'm no seer...'

The Baptist's face clouded for a moment, then he laughed awkwardly. 'Say nothing. Eat with me tonight. I have wild-honey and locusts.'

Glogauer had not yet eaten this food, which was the staple of travellers who did not carry provisions but lived off the food they could find on the journey. Some regarded it as a delicacy.

He tried it later, as he sat in John's house. There were only two rooms in the house. One was for eating, the other for sleeping in. The honey and locusts was too sweet for his taste, but it was a welcome change from barley or goat-meat.

He sat cross-legged, opposite John the Baptist who ate with relish. Night had fallen. From outside came low murmurs and the moans and cries of those at prayer.

Glogauer dipped another locust into the bowl of honey that rested between them. 'Do you plan to lead the people of Judaea in revolt against the Romans?' he asked.

The Baptist seemed disturbed by the direct question. It was the first of its nature that Glogauer had put to him.

'If it be Adonai's will,' he said, not looking up as he leant towards the bowl of honey.

'The Romans know this?'

'I do not know, Emmanuel, but Herod the incestuous has doubtless told them I speak against the unrighteous.'

'Yet the Romans do not arrest you.'

'Pilate dare not – not since the petition was sent to the Emperor Tiberius.'

'Petition?'

'Aye, the one that Herod and the Pharisees signed when Pilate the procurator did place votive shields in the palace at Jerusalem and seek to violate the Temple. Tiberius rebuked

Pilate and since then, though he still hates the Jews, the procurator is more careful in his treatment of us.'

'Tell me, John, do you know how long Tiberius has ruled in Rome?' He had not had the chance to ask that question again until now.

'Fourteen years.'

It was AD 28; something less than a year before the crucifixion would take place, and his time machine was smashed.

Now John the Baptist planned armed rebellion against the occupying Romans, but, if the Gospels were to be believed, would soon be decapitated by Herod. Certainly no large-scale rebellion had taken place at this time. Even those who claimed that the entry of Jesus and his disciples into Jerusalem and the invasion of the Temple were plainly the actions of armed rebels had found no records to suggest that John had led a similar revolt.

Glogauer had come to like the Baptist very much. The man was plainly a hardened revolutionary who had been planning revolt against the Romans for years and had slowly been building up enough followers to make the attempt successful. He reminded Glogauer strongly of the resistance leaders of the Second World War. He had a similar toughness and understanding of the realities of his position. He knew that he would only have one chance to smash the cohorts garrisoned in the country. If the revolt became protracted, Rome would have ample time to send more troops to Jerusalem.

When do you think Adonai intends to destroy the unrighteous through your agency?' Glogauer said tactfully.

John glanced at him with some amusement. He smiled. 'The Passover is a time when the people are restless and resent the strangers most,' he said.

'When is the next Passover?'

'Not for many months.'

'How can I help you?'

'You are a magus.'

'I can work no miracles.'

John wiped the honey from his beard. 'I cannot believe that, Emmanuel. The manner of your coming was miraculous. The Essenes did not know if you were a devil or a messenger from Adonai.'

'I am neither.'

'Why do you confuse me, Emmanuel? I know that you are Adonai's messenger. You are the sign that the Essenes sought.

The time is almost ready. The kingdom of heaven shall soon be established on earth. Come with me. Tell the people that you speak with Adonai's voice. Work mighty miracles.'

'Your power is waning, is that it?' Glogauer looked sharply at John. 'You need me to renew your rebels' hopes?'

'You speak like a Roman, with such lack of subtlety.' John got up angrily. Evidently, like the Essenes he lived with, he preferred less direct conversation. There was a practical reason for this, Glogauer realized, in that John and his men feared betrayal all the time. Even the Essenes' records were partially written in cypher, with one innocent-seeming word or phrase meaning something else entirely.

'I am sorry, John. But tell me if I am right.' Glogauer spoke softly.

'Are you not a magus, coming in that chariot from nowhere?' The Baptist waved his hands and shrugged his shoulders. 'My men saw you! They saw the shining thing take shape in air, crack and let you enter out of it. Is that not magical? The clothing you wore – was that earthly raiment? The talismans within the chariot – did they not speak of powerful magic? The prophet said that a magus would come from Egypt and be called Emmanuel. So it is written in the Book of Micah! Are none of these things true?'

'Most of them. But there are explanations –' he broke off, unable to think of the nearest word to 'rational'. 'I am an ordinary man, like you. I have no power to work miracles! I am just a man!'

John glowered. 'You mean you refuse to help us?'

'I'm grateful to you and the Essenes. You saved my life almost certainly. If I can repay that...'

John nodded his head deliberately. 'You can repay it, Emmanuel.'

'How?'

'Be the great magus I need. Let me present you to all those who become impatient and would turn away from Adonai's will. Let me tell them the manner of your coming to us. Then you can say that all is Adonai's will and that they must prepare to accomplish it.'

John stared at him intensely.

'Will you, Emmanuel?'

'For your sake, John. And in turn, will you send men to bring my chariot here as soon as possible. I wish to see if it may be mended.'

'I will.'

Glogauer felt exhilarated. He began to laugh. The Baptist looked at him with slight bewilderment. Then he began to join in.

Glogauer laughed on. History would not mention it, but he, with John the Baptist, would prepare the way for Christ.

Christ was not born yet. Perhaps Glogauer knew it, one year before the crucifixion.

And the Word was made flesh, and dwelt among us (and we beheld his glory, the glory as of the only begotten of the Father) full of grace and truth. John bare witness of him, and cried, saying, This was he of whom I spake, He that cometh after me is preferred before me: for he was before me.

(John 1:14–15)

Even when he had first met Monica they had had long arguments. His father had not then died and left him the money to buy the Occult Bookshop in Great Russell Street, opposite the British Museum. He was doing all sorts of temporary work and his spirits were very low. At that time Monica had seemed a great help, a great guide through the mental darkness engulfing him. They had both lived close to Holland Park and went there for walks almost every Sunday of the summer of 1962. At twenty-two, he was already obsessed with Jung's strange brand of Christian mysticism. She, who despised Jung, had soon begun to denigrate all his ideas. She never really convinced him, but, after a while, she had succeeded in confusing him. It would be another six months before they went to bed together.

It was uncomfortably hot.

They sat in the shade of the cafeteria, watching a distant cricket match. Nearer to them, two girls and a boy sat on the grass, drinking orange squash from plastic cups. One of the girls had a guitar across her lap and she set the cup down and began to play, singing a folksong in a high, gentle voice. Glogauer tried to listen to the words. As a student, he had always liked traditional folk music.

'Christianity is dead.' Monica sipped her tea. 'Religion is dying. God was killed in 1945.'

'There may yet be a resurrection,' he said.

'Let us hope not. Religion was the creation of fear. Knowledge destroys fear. Without fear, religion can't survive.'

'You think there's no fear about these days?'

'Not the same kind, Karl.'

'Haven't you ever considered the *idea* of Christ?' he asked her, changing his tack. 'What that means to Christians?'

'The idea of the tractor means as much to a Marxist,' she replied.

'But what came first? The idea or the actuality of Christ?'

She shrugged. 'The actuality, if it matters. Jesus was a Jewish troublemaker organizing a revolt against the Romans. He was crucified for his pains. That's all we know and all we need to know.'

'A great religion couldn't have begun so simply.'

'When people need one, they'll make a great religion out of the most unlikely beginnings.'

'That's my point, Monica.' He gesticulated at her and she drew away slightly. 'The *idea* preceded the *actuality* of Christ.'

'Oh, Karl, don't go on. The actuality of *Jesus* preceded the idea of *Christ*.'

A couple walked past, glancing at them as they argued.

Monica noticed them and fell silent. She got up and he rose as well, but she shook her head. 'I'm going home, Karl. You stay here. I'll see you in a few days.'

He watched her walk down the wide path towards the park gates.

The next day, when he got home from work, he found a letter. She must have written it after she had left him and posted it the same day.

Dear Karl,

Conversation doesn't seem to have much effect on you, you know. It's as if you listen to the tone of the voice, the rhythm of the words, without ever hearing what is trying to be communicated. You're a bit like a sensitive animal who can't understand what's being said to it, but can tell if the person talking is pleased or angry and so on. That's why I'm writing to you – to try to get my idea across. You respond too emotionally when we're together.

You make the mistake of considering Christianity as something that developed over the course of a few years, from the death of Jesus to the time the Gospels were written. But Christianity wasn't new. Only the name was new. Christianity was merely a stage in the meeting, cross-fertilization metamorphosis of Western logic and Eastern mysticism. Look how the religion itself changed over the centuries, re-interpreting itself to meet changing times. Christianity is just a new name for a conglomeration of old myths and philosophies. All the Gospels do is retell the sun myth and garble some of the ideas from the Greeks and Romans. Even in the second century, Jewish scholars were showing it up for the mish-mash it was! They pointed out the strong similarities between the various sun myths and the Christ myth. The miracles didn't happen – they were invented later, borrowed from here and there.

Remember the old Victorians who used to say that Plato was really a Christian because he anticipated Christian thought? Christian thought! Christianity was a vehicle for ideas in circulation for centuries before Christ. Was Marcus Aurelius a Christian? He was writing in the direct tradition of Western philosophy. That's why Christianity caught on in Europe and not in the East! You should have been a theologian with your bias, not a psychiatrist. The same goes for your friend Jung.

Try to clear your head of all this morbid nonsense and you'll be a lot better at your job.

Yours,
Monica.

He screwed the letter up and threw it away. Later that evening he was tempted to look at it again, but resisted the temptation.

CHAPTER THREE

John stood up to his waist in the river. Most of the Essenes stood on the banks watching him. Glogauer looked down at him.

'I cannot, John. It is not for me to do it.'

The Baptist muttered. 'You must.'

Glogauer shivered as he lowered himself into the river beside the Baptist. He felt light-headed. He stood there trembling, unable to move.

His foot slipped on the rocks of the river and John reached out and gripped his arm, steadying him.

In the clear sky, the sun was at zenith, beating down on his unprotected head.

'Emmanuel!' John cried suddenly. 'The spirit of Adonai is within you!'

Glogauer still found it hard to speak. He shook his head slightly. It was aching and he could hardly see. Today he was having his first migraine attack since he had come here. He wanted to vomit. John's voice sounded distant.

He swayed in the water.

As he began to fall towards the Baptist, the whole scene around him shimmered. He felt John catch him and heard himself say desperately: 'John, baptize *me*!' And then there was water in his mouth and throat and he was coughing.

John's voice was crying something. Whatever the words were, they drew a response from the people on both banks. The roaring in his ears increased, its quality changing. He thrashed in the water, then felt himself lifted to his feet.

The Essenes were swaying in unison, every face lifted upwards towards the glaring sun.

Glogauer began to vomit into the water, stumbling as John's hands gripped his arms painfully and guided him up the bank.

A peculiar, rhythmic humming came from the mouths of the Essenes as they swayed; it rose as they swayed to one side, fell as they swayed to the other.

Glogauer covered his ears as John released him. He was still retching, but it was dry now, and worse than before.

He began to stagger away, barely keeping his balance, running, with his ears still covered; running over the rocky scrubland; running as the sun throbbed in the sky and its heat pounded at his head; running away.

But John forbad him, saying, I have need to be baptized of thee, and comest thou to me? And Jesus answering said unto him, Suffer it to be so now: for thus it becometh us to fulfil all righteousness. Then he suffered him. And Jesus, when he was baptized, went up straightway out of the water: and, lo, the heavens were opened unto him, and he saw the Spirit of God descending like a dove, and lighting upon him: and lo a voice from heaven, saying, This is my beloved Son, in whom I am well pleased.

(Matthew 3:14–17)

He had been fifteen, doing well at the grammar school. He had read in the newspapers about the Teddy Boy gangs that roamed South London, but the odd youth he had seen in pseudo-Edwardian clothes had seemed harmless and stupid enough.

He had gone to the pictures in Brixton Hill and decided to walk home to Streatham because he had spent most of the bus money on an ice-cream. They came out of the cinema at the same time. He hardly noticed them as they followed him down the hill.

Then, quite suddenly, they had surrounded him. Pale, mean-faced boys, most of them a year or two older than he was. He realized that he knew two of them vaguely. They were at the big council school in the same street as the grammar school. They used the same football ground.

'Hello,' he said weakly.

'Hello, son,' said the oldest Teddy Boy. He was chewing gum, standing with one knee bent, grinning at him. 'Where you going, then?'

'Home.'

'Heouwm,' said the biggest one, imitating his accent. 'What are you going to do when you get there?'

'Go to bed.' Karl tried to get through the ring, but they wouldn't let him. They pressed him back into a shop doorway. Beyond them, cars droned by on the main road. The street was brightly lit, with street lamps and neon from the shops. Several people passed, but none of them stopped. Karl began to feel panic.

'Got no homework to do, son?' said the boy next to the leader. He was red-headed and freckled and his eyes were a hard grey.

'Want to fight one of us?' another boy asked. It was one of the boys he knew.

'No, I don't fight. Let me go.'

'You scared, son?' said the leader, grinning. Ostentatiously, he pulled a streamer of gum from his mouth and then replaced it. He began chewing again.

'No. Why should I want to fight you?'

'You reckon you're better than us, is that it, son?'

'No.' He was beginning to tremble. Tears were coming into his eyes. ' 'Course not.'

' 'Course not, son.'

He moved forward again, but they pushed him back into the doorway.

'You're the bloke with the kraut name ain't you?' said the

other boy he knew. 'Glow-worm or something.'

'Glogauer. Let me go.'

'Won't your mummy like it if you're back late?'

'More a yid name than a kraut name.'

'You a yid, son?'

'He looks like a yid.'

'You a yid, son?'

'You a Jewish boy, son?'

'You a yid, son?'

'Shut up!' Karl screamed. He pushed into them. One of them punched him in the stomach. He grunted with pain. Another pushed him and he staggered.

People were still hurrying by on the pavement. They glanced at the group as they went past. One man stopped, but his wife pulled him on. 'Just some kids larking about,' she said.

'Get his trousers down,' one of the boys suggested with a laugh. 'That'll prove it.'

Karl pushed through them and this time they didn't resist. He began to run down the hill.

'Give him a start,' he heard one of the boys say.

He ran on.

They began to follow him, laughing.

They did not catch up with him by the time he turned into the avenue where he lived. He reached the house and ran along the dark passage beside it. He opened the back door. His stepmother was in the kitchen.

'What's the matter with you?' she said.

She was a tall, thin woman; nervous and hysterical. Her dark hair was untidy.

He went past her into the breakfast-room.

'What's the matter, Karl?' she called. Her voice was high-pitched.

'Nothing,' he said.

He didn't want a scene.

It was cold when he woke up. The false dawn was grey and he could see nothing but barren country in all directions. He could not remember a great deal about the previous day, except that he had run a long way.

Dew had gathered on his loincloth. He wet his lips and rubbed the skin over his face. As he always did after a migraine attack he felt weak and completely drained. Looking down at his naked body, he noticed how skinny he had become. Life with the Essenes had caused that, of course.

He wondered why he had panicked so much when John had asked him to baptize him. Was it simply honesty – something in him which resisted deceiving the Essenes into thinking he was a prophet of some kind? It was hard to know.

He wrapped the goatskin about his hips and tied it tightly just above his left thigh. He supposed he had better try to get back to the camp and find John and apologize, see if he could make amends.

The time machine was there now, too. They had dragged it there, using only rawhide ropes.

If a good blacksmith could be found, or some other metal-worker, there was just a chance that it could be repaired. The journey back would be dangerous.

He wondered if he ought to go back right away, or try to shift to a time nearer to the actual crucifixion. He had not gone back specifically to witness the crucifixion, but to get the mood of Jerusalem during the Feast of the Passover, when Jesus was supposed to have entered the city. Monica had thought Jesus had stormed the city with an armed band. She had said that all the evidence pointed to that. All the evidence of one sort did point to it, but he could not accept the evidence. There was more to it, he was sure. If only he could meet Jesus. John had apparently never heard of him, though he had told Glogauer that there was a prophecy that the Messiah would be a Nazarene. There were many prophecies, and many of them conflicted.

He began to walk back in the general direction of the Essene camp. He could not have come so far. He would soon recognize the hills where they had their caves.

Soon it was very hot and the ground more barren. The air wavered before his eyes. The feeling of exhaustion with which he had awakened increased. His mouth was dry and his legs were weak. He was hungry and there was nothing to eat. There was no sign of the range of hills where the Essenes had their camp.

There was one hill, about two miles away to the south. He decided to make for it. From there he would probably be able to get his bearings, perhaps even see a township where they would give him food.

The sandy soil turned to floating dust around him as his feet disturbed it. A few primitive shrubs clung to the ground and jutting rocks tripped him.

He was bleeding and bruised by the time he began, painfully, to clamber up the hillside.

The journey to the summit (which was much further away than he had originally judged) was difficult. He would slide on the loose stones of the hillside, falling on his face, bracing his torn hands and feet to stop himself from sliding down to the bottom, clinging to tufts of grass and lichen that grew here and there, embracing larger projections of rock when he could, resting frequently, his mind and body both numb with pain and weariness.

He sweated beneath the sun. The dust stuck to the moisture on his half-naked body, caking him from head to foot. The goatskin was in shreds.

The barren world reeled around him, sky somehow merging with land, yellow rock with white clouds. Nothing seemed still.

He reached the summit and lay there gasping. Everything had become unreal.

He heard Monica's voice, thought he glanced her for a moment from the corner of his eye.

Don't be melodramatic, Karl . . .

She had said that many times. His own voice replied now.

I'm born out of my time, Monica. This age of reason has no place for me. It will kill me in the end.

Her voice replied.

Guilt and fear and your own masochism. You could be a brilliant psychiatrist, but you've given in to all your own neuroses so completely . . .

'Shut up!'

He rolled over on his back. The sun blazed down on his tattered body.

'Shut up!'

The whole Christian syndrome, Karl. You'll become a Catholic convert next I shouldn't doubt. Where's your strength of mind?

'Shut up! Go away, Monica.'

Fear shapes your thoughts. You're not searching for a soul or even a meaning for life. You're searching for comforts.

'Leave me alone, Monica!'

His grimy hands covered his ears. His hair and beard were matted with dust. Blood had congealed on the minor wounds that were now on every part of his body. Above, the sun seemed to pound in unison with his heartbeats.

You're going downhill, Karl, don't you realize that? Downhill. Pull yourself together. You're not entirely incapable of rational thought...

'Oh, Monica! Shut up!'

His voice was harsh and cracked. A few ravens circled the sky above him now. He heard them calling back at him in a voice not unlike his own.

God died in 1945...

'It isn't 1945 – it's AD 28. God is alive!'

How you can bother to wonder about an obvious syncretistic religion like Christianity – Rabbinic Judaism, Stoic ethics, Greek mystery cults, Oriental ritual...

'It doesn't matter!'

Not to you in your present state of mind.

'I need God!'

That's what it boils down to, doesn't it? Okay, Karl, carve your own crutches. Just think what you could have been if you'd have come to terms with yourself...

Glogauer pulled his ruined body to its feet and stood on the summit of the hill and screamed.

The ravens were startled. They wheeled in the sky and flew away.

The sky was darkening now.

Then was Jesus led up of the Spirit into the wilderness to be tempted of the devil. And when he had fasted forty days and forty nights, he was afterward an hungred.

(Matthew 4:1–2)

CHAPTER FOUR

The madman came stumbling into the town. His feet stirred the dust and made it dance and dogs barked around him as he walked mechanically, his head turned upwards to face the sun, his arms limp at his sides, his lips moving.

To the townspeople, the words they heard were in familiar language; yet they were uttered with such intensity and conviction that God himself might be using this emaciated, naked creature as his spokesman.

They wondered where the madman had come from.

The white town consisted primarily of double- and single-storeyed houses of stone and clay-brick, built around a market place that was fronted by an ancient, simple synagogue outside which old men sat and talked, dressed in dark robes. The town was prosperous and clean, thriving on Roman commerce. Only one or two beggars were in the streets and these were well-fed. The streets followed the rise and fall of the hillside on which they were built. They were winding streets, shady and peaceful; country streets. There was a smell of newly-cut timber everywhere in the air, and the sound of carpentry, for the town was chiefly famous for its skilled carpenters. It lay on the edge of the Plain of Jezreel, close to the trade route between Damascus and Egypt, and wagons were always leaving it, laden with the work of the town's craftsmen. The town was called Nazareth.

The madman had found it by asking every traveller he saw where it was. He had passed through other towns – Philadelphia, Gerasa, Pella and Scythopolis, following the Roman roads – asking the same question in his outlandish accent. 'Where lies Nazareth?'

Some had given him food on the way. Some had asked for his blessing and he had laid hands on them, speaking in that strange tongue. Some had pelted him with stones and driven him away.

He had crossed the Jordan by the Roman viaduct and continued northwards towards Nazareth.

There had been no difficulty in finding the town, but it had been difficult for him to force himself towards it. He had lost a great deal of blood and had eaten very little on the journey. He would walk until he collapsed and lie there until he could go on, or, as had happened increasingly, until someone found him and had given him a little sour wine or bread to revive him.

Once some Roman legionaries had stopped and with brusque kindness asked him if he had any relatives they could take him to. They had addressed him in pidgin-Aramaic and had been surprised when he replied in a strangely-accented Latin that was purer than the language they spoke themselves.

They asked him if he were a Rabbi or a scholar. He told them he was neither. The officer of the legionaries had offered him some dried meat and wine. The men were part of a patrol that passed this way once a month. They were stocky, brown-faced men, with hard, clean-shaven faces. They were dressed in stained leather kilts and breastplates and sandles, and had iron helmets on their heads, scabbarded short swords at their hips. Even as they stood around him in the evening sunlight they did not seem relaxed. The officer, softer-voiced than his men but otherwise much like them save that he wore a metal breastplate and a long cloak, asked the madman what his name was.

For a moment the madman had paused, his mouth opening and closing, as if he could remember what he was called.

'Karl,' he said at length, doubtfully. It was more a suggestion than a statement.

'Sounds almost like a Roman name,' said one of the legionaries.

'Are you a citizen?' the officer asked.

But the madman's mind was wandering, evidently. He looked away from them, muttering to himself.

All at once, he looked back at them and said: 'Nazareth?'

'That way.' The officer pointed down the road that cut between the hills. 'Are you a Jew?'

This seemed to startle the madman. He sprang to his feet and tried to push through the soldiers. They let him through, laughing. He was a harmless madman.

They watched him run down the road.

'One of their prophets, perhaps,' said the officer, walking towards his horse. The country was full of them. Every other man you met claimed to be spreading the message of their god. They didn't make much trouble and religion seemed to keep their minds off rebellion. We should be grateful, thought the officer.

His men were still laughing.

They began to march down the road in the opposite direction to the one the madman had taken.

Now the madman was in Nazareth and the townspeople looked at him with curiosity and more than a little suspicion as he staggered into the market square. He could be a wandering prophet or he could be possessed by devils. It was often hard to tell. The rabbis would know.

As he passed the knots of people standing by the merchants' stalls, they fell silent until he had gone by. Women pulled their heavy woollen shawls about their well-fed bodies and men tucked in their cotton robes so that he would not touch them. Normally their instinct would have been to have taxed him with his business in the town, but there was an intensity about his gaze, a quickness and vitality about his face, in spite of his emaciated appearance, that made them treat him with some respect and they kept their distance.

When he reached the centre of the market place, he stopped and looked around him. He seemed slow to notice the people. He blinked and licked his lips.

A woman passed, eyeing him warily. He spoke to her, his voice soft, the words carefully formed. 'Is this Nazareth?'

'It is.' She nodded and increased her pace.

A man was crossing the square. He was dressed in a woollen robe of red and brown stripes. There was a red skull cap on his curly, black hair. His face was plump and cheerful. The madman walked across the man's path and stopped him. 'I seek a carpenter.'

'There are many carpenters in Nazareth. The town is famous for its carpenters. I am a carpenter myself. Can I help you?' The man's voice was good-humoured, patronizing.

'Do you know a carpenter called Joseph? A descendant of David. He has a wife called Mary and several children. One is named Jesus.'

The cheerful man screwed his face into a mock frown and scratched the back of his neck. 'I know more than one Joseph. There is one poor fellow in yonder street.' He pointed. 'He has a wife called Mary. Try there. You should soon find him. Look for a man who never laughs.'

The madman looked in the direction in which the man pointed. As soon as he saw the street, he seemed to forget everything else and strode towards it.

In the narrow street he entered the smell of cut timber was even stronger. He walked ankle-deep in wood-shavings. From every building came the thud of hammers, the scrape of saws. There were planks of all sizes resting against the pale, shaded walls of the houses and there was hardly room to pass between them. Many of the carpenters had their benches just outside the doors. They were carving bowls, operating simple lathes, shaping wood into everything imaginable. They looked up as the madman entered the street and approached one old carpenter in a leather apron who sat at his bench carving a figurine. The man had grey hair and seemed short-sighted. He peered up at the madman.

'What do you want?'

'I seek a carpenter called Joseph. He has a wife – Mary.'

The old man gestured with the hand that held the half-completed figurine. 'Two houses along on the other side of the street.'

The house the madman came to had very few planks leaning against it, and the quality of the timber seemed poorer than the other wood he had seen. The bench near the entrance was warped on one side and the man who sat hunched over it repairing a stool seemed misshapen also. He straightened up as the madman touched his shoulder. His face was lined and pouched with misery. His eyes were tired and his thin beard had premature streaks of grey. He coughed slightly, perhaps in surprise at being disturbed.

'Are you Joseph?' asked the madman.

'I've no money.'

'I want nothing – just to ask a few questions.'

'I'm Joseph. Why do you want to know?'

'Have you a son?'

'Several, and daughters, too.'

'Your wife is called Mary? You are of David's line.'

The man waved his hand impatiently. 'Yes, for what good either have done me...'

'I wish to meet one of your sons. Jesus. Can you tell me where he is?'

'That good-for-nothing. What has he done now?'

'Where is he?'

Jospeh's eyes became more calculating as he stared at the madman. 'Are you a seer of some kind? Have you come to cure my son?'

'I am a prophet of sorts. I can foretell the future.'

Joseph got up with a sigh. 'You can see him. Come.' He led the madman through the gateway into the cramped courtyard of the house. It was crowded with pieces of wood, broken furniture and implements, rotting sacks of shavings. They entered the darkened house. In the first room – evidently a kitchen – a woman stood by a large clay stove. She was tall and bulging with fat. Her long, black hair was unbound and greasy, falling over large, lustrous eyes that still had the heat of sensuality. She looked the madman over.

'There's no food for beggars,' she grunted. 'He eats enough as it is.' She gestured with a wooden spoon at a small figure sitting in the shadow of a corner. The figure shifted as she spoke.

'He seeks our Jesus,' said Joseph to the woman. 'Perhaps he

comes to ease our burden.'

The woman gave the madman a sidelong look and shrugged. She licked her red lips with a fat tongue. 'Jesus!'

The figure in the corner stood up.

'That's him,' said the woman with a certain satisfaction.

The madman frowned, shaking his head rapidly. 'No.'

The figure was misshapen. It had a pronounced hunched back and a cast in its left eye. The face was vacant and foolish. There was a little spittle on the lips. It giggled as its name was repeated. It took a crooked step forward. 'Jesus,' it said. The word was slurred and thick. 'Jesus.'

'That's all he can say.' The woman sneered. 'He's always been like that.'

'God's judgement,' said Joseph bitterly.

'What is wrong with him?' There was a pathetic, desperate note in the madman's voice.

'He's always been like that.' The woman turned back to the stove. 'You can have him if you want him. Addled inside and outside. I was carrying him when my parents married me off to that half-man . . .'

'You shameless –' Joseph stopped as his wife glared at him. He turned to the madman. 'What's your business with our son?'

'I wished to talk to him. I . . .'

'He's no oracle – no seer – we used to think he might be. There are still people in Nazareth who come to him to cure them or tell their fortunes, but he only giggles at them and speaks his name over and over again . . .'

'Are – you sure – there is not – something about him – you have not noticed?'

'Sure!' Mary snorted sardonically. 'We need money badly enough. If he had any magical powers, we'd know.'

Jesus giggled again and limped away into another room.

'It is impossible,' the madman murmured. Could history itself have changed? Could he be in some other dimension of time where Christ had never been?

Joseph appeared to notice the look of agony in the madman's eyes.

'What is it?' he said. 'What do you see? You said you foretold the future. Tell us how we will fare?'

'Not *now*,' said the prophet, turning away. 'Not *now*.'

He ran from the house and down the street with its smell of planed oak, cedar, and cypress. He ran back to the market place and stopped, looking wildly about him. He saw the synagogue directly ahead of him. He began to walk towards it.

The man he had spoken to earlier was still in the market place, buying cooking pots to give to his daughter as a wedding gift. He nodded towards the strange man as he entered the synagogue. 'He's a relative of Joseph the carpenter,' he told the man beside him. 'A prophet, I shouldn't wonder.'

The madman, the prophet, Karl Glogauer, the time-traveller, the neurotic psychiatrist manqué, the searcher for meaning, the masochist, the man with a death-wish, and the messiah-complex, the anachronism, made his way into the synagogue gasping for breath. He had seen the man he had sought. He had seen Jesus, the son of Joseph and Mary. He had seen a man he recognized without any doubt as a congenital imbecile.

'All men have a messiah-complex, Karl,' Monica had said.

The memories were less complete now. His sense of time and identity was becoming confused.

'There were dozens of messiahs in Galilee at the time. That Jesus should have been the one to carry the myth and the philosophy was a coincidence of history...'

'There must have been more to it than that, Monica.'

Every Tuesday in the room above the Occult Bookshop, the Jungian discussion group would meet for purposes of group analysis and therapy. Glogauer had not organized the group, but he had willingly lent his premises to it and had joined it eagerly. It was a great relief to talk with like-minded people once a week. One of his reasons for buying the Occult Bookshop was so that he would meet interesting people like those who attended the Jungian discussion group.

An obsession with Jung brought them together, but everyone had special obsessions of their own. Mrs Rita Blenn charted the courses of flying saucers, though it was not clear if she believed in them or not. Hugh Joyce believed that all Jungian archetypes derived from the original race of Atlanteans who had perished millennia before. Alan Cheddar, the youngest of the group, was interested in Indian mysticism, and Sandra Peterson, the organizer, was a great witchcraft specialist. James Headington was interested in time. He was the group's pride; he was Sir James Headington, war-time inventor, very rich and with all sorts of decorations for his contribution to the Allied victory. He had had the reputation of being a great improviser during the war, but after it he had become something of an embarrassment to the War Office. He was a crank, they thought, and what was worse, he aired his crankiness in public.

Every so often, Sir James would tell the other members of the group about his time machine. They humoured him. Most of them were liable to exaggerate their own experiences connected with their different interests.

One Tuesday evening, after everyone else had left, Headington told Glogauer that his machine was ready.

'I can't believe it,' Glogauer said truthfully.

'You're the first person I've told.'

'Why me?'

'I don't know. I like you – and the shop.'

'You haven't told the government.'

Headington had chuckled. 'Why should I? Not until I've tested it fully, anyway. Serves them right for putting me out to pasture.'

'You don't know it works?'

'I'm sure it does. Would you like to see it?'

'A time machine.' Glogauer smiled weakly.'

'Come and see it.'

'Why me?'

'I thought you might be interested. I know you don't hold with the orthodox view of science...'

Glogauer felt sorry for him.

'Come and see,' said Headington.

He went down to Banbury the next day. The same day he left 1976 and arrived in AD 28.

The synagogue was cool and quiet with a subtle scent of incense. The rabbis guided him into the courtyard. They, like the townspeople, did not know what to make of him, but they were sure it was not a devil that possessed him. It was their custom to give shelter to the roaming prophets who were now everywhere in Galilee, though this one was stranger than the rest. His face was immobile and his body was stiff, and there were tears running down his dirty cheeks. They had never seen such agony in a man's eyes before.

'Science can say how, but it never asks why,' he had told Monica. 'It can't answer.'

'Who wants to know?' she'd replied.

'I do.'

'Well, you'll never find out, will you?'

'Sit down, my son,' said the rabbi. 'What do you wish to ask of us?'

'Where is Christ?' he said. 'Where is Christ?'

They did not understand the language.

'Is it Greek?' asked one, but another shook his head.

Kyrios: The Lord.

Adonai: The Lord.

Where was the Lord?

He frowned, looking vaguely about him.

'I must rest,' he said in their language.

'Where are you from?'

He could not think what to answer.

'Where are you from?' a rabbi repeated.

'Ha-Olam Hab-Bah . . .' he murmured at length.

They looked at one another. '*Ha- Olam Hab-Bah,*' they said.

Ha-Olam Hab-Bah; Ha-Olam Haz-Zeh: The world to come and the world that is.

'Do you bring us a message?' said one of the rabbis. They were used to prophets, certainly, but none like this one. 'A message?'

'I do not know,' said the prophet hoarsely. 'I must rest. I am hungry.'

'Come. We will give you food and a place to sleep.'

He could only eat a little of the rich food and the bed with its straw-stuffed mattress was too soft for him. He was not used to it.

He slept badly, shouting as he dreamed, and, outside the room, the rabbis listened, but could understand little of what he said.

Karl Glogauer stayed in the synagogue for several weeks. He would spend most of his time reading in the library, searching through the long scrolls for some answer to his dilemma. The words of the Testaments, in many cases capable of a dozen interpretations, only confused him further. There was nothing to grasp, nothing to tell him what had gone wrong.

The rabbis kept their distance for the most part. They had accepted him as a holy man. They were proud to have him in their synagogue. They were sure that he was one of the special chosen of God and they waited patiently for him to speak to them.

But the prophet said little, muttering only to himself in snatches of their own language and snatches of the incomprehensible language he often used, even when he addressed them directly.

In Nazareth, the townsfolk talked of little else but the mysterious prophet in the synagogue, but the rabbis would not answer their questions. They would tell the people to go about their business, that there were things they were not yet meant to know. In this way, as priests had always done, they avoided questions they could not answer while at the same time appearing to have much more knowledge than they actually possessed.

Then, one sabbath, he appeared in the public part of the synagogue and took his place with the others who had come to worship.

The man who was reading from the scroll on his left stumbled over the words, glancing at the prophet from the corner of his eye.

The prophet sat and listened, his expression remote.

The Chief Rabbi looked uncertainly at him, then signed that the scroll should be passed to the prophet. This was done hesitantly by a boy who placed the scroll into the prophet's hands.

The prophet looked at the words for a long time and then began to read. The prophet read without comprehending at first what he read. It was the book of Esaias.

> *The Spirit of the Lord is upon me, because he hath anointed me to preach the gospel to the poor; he hath sent me to heal the brokenhearted, to preach deliverance to the captives, and recovering of sight to the blind, to set at liberty them that are bruised, to preach the acceptable year of the Lord. And he closed the book, and gave it again to the minister, and sat down. And the eyes of all of them that were in the synagogue were fastened on him.*
>
> (Luke 4:18–20)

CHAPTER FIVE

They followed him now, as he walked away from Nazareth towards the Lake of Galilee. He was dressed in the white linen robe they had given him and though they thought he led them, they, in fact, drove him before them.

'He is our messiah,' they said to those that inquired. And there were already rumours of miracles.

When he saw the sick, he pitied them and tried to do what he could because they expected something of them. Many he could do nothing for, but others, obviously in psychosomatic conditions, he could help. They believed in his power more strongly than they believed in their sickness. So he cured them.

When he came to Capernaum, some fifty people followed him into the streets of the city. It was already known that he was in some way associated with John the Baptist, who enjoyed huge prestige in Galilee and had been declared a true prophet by many Pharisees. Yet this man had a power greater, in some ways, than John's. He was not the orator that the Baptist was, but he had worked miracles.

Capernaum was a sprawling town beside the crystal lake of Galilee, its houses separated by large market gardens. Fishing boats were moored at the white quayside, as well as trading ships that plied the lakeside towns. Though the green hills came down from all sides to the lake, Capernaum itself was built on flat ground, sheltered by the hills. It was a quiet town and, like most others in Galilee, had a large population of gentiles, Greek, Roman, and Egyptian traders walked its streets and many had made permanent homes there. There was a prosperous middle-class of merchants, artisans, and ship-owners, as well as doctors, lawyers, and scholars, for Capernaum was on the borders of the provinces of Galilee, Trachonitis, and Syria and though a comparatively small town was a useful junction for trade and travel.

The strange, mad prophet in his swirling linen robes, followed by the heterogeneous crowd that was primarily composed of poor folk but also could be seen to contain men of some distinction, swept into Capernaum. The news spread that this man really could foretell the future, that he had already predicted the arrest of John by Herod Antipas and soon after Herod had imprisoned the Baptist at Peraea. He did not make the predictions in general terms, using vague words the way other prophets did. He spoke of things that were to happen in the near future and he spoke of them in detail.

None knew his name. He was simply the prophet from Nazareth, or the Nazarene. Some said he was a relative, perhaps the son, of a carpenter in Nazareth, but this could be because the written words for 'son of a carpenter' and 'magus' were almost the same and the confusion had come about in that way. There was even a very faint rumour that his name was Jesus. The name had been used once or twice, but when they asked him if that was, indeed, his name, he denied it or else, in his abstracted way, refused to answer at all.

His actual preaching tended to lack the fire of John's. This man spoke gently, rather vaguely, and smiled often. He spoke of God in a strange way, too, and he appeared to be connected, as John was, with the Essenes, for he preached against the accumulation of personal wealth and spoke of mankind as a brotherhood, as they did.

But it was the miracles that they watched for as he was guided to the graceful synagogue of Capernaum. No prophet before him had healed the sick and seemed to understand the troubles that people rarely spoke of. It was his sympathy that they responded to, rather than the words he spoke.

For the first time in his life, Karl Glogauer had forgotten about Karl Glogauer. For the first time in his life he was doing what he had always sought to do as a psychiatrist.

But it was not his life. He was bringing a myth to life – a generation before that myth would be born. He was completing a certain kind of psychic circuit. He was not changing history, but he was giving history more substance.

He could not bear to think that Jesus had been nothing more than a myth. It was in his power to make Jesus a physical reality rather than the creation of a process of mythogenesis.

So he spoke in the synagogues and he spoke of a gentler God than any most of them had heard of, and where he could remember them, he told them parables.

And gradually the need to justify what he was doing faded and his sense of identity grew increasingly more tenuous and was replaced by a different sense of identity, where he gave greater and greater substance of the role he had chosen. It was an archetypal role. It was a role to appeal to a disciple of Jung. It was a role that went beyond a mere imitation. It was a role that he must now play out to the very last grand detail. Karl Glogauer had discovered the reality he had been seeking.

And in the synagogue there was a man, which had a spirit of an unclean devil, and cried out with a loud voice, saying, Let us alone; what have we to do with thee, thou Jesus of Nazareth? art thou come to destroy us? I know thee who thou art; the Holy One of God. And Jesus rebuked him, saying, Hold thy peace, and come out of him. And when the devil had thrown him in the midst, he came out of him, and hurt him not. And they were all amazed, and spake among themselves, saying. What a word is this! for with authority and power he commandeth the unclean spirits, and they come out. And the fame of him went out into every place of the country round about.

(Luke 4:33–37)

'Mass hallucination. Miracles, flying saucers, ghosts, it's all the same,' Monica had said.

'Very likely,' he had replied. 'But *why* did they see them?'

'Because they wanted to.'

'Why did they want to?'

'Because they were afraid.'

'You think that's all there is to it?'

'Isn't it enough?'

When he left Capernaum for the first time, many more people accompanied him. It had become impractical to stay in the town, for the business of the town had been brought almost to a standstill by the crowds that sought to see him work his simple miracles.

He spoke to them in the spaces beyond the towns. He talked with intelligent, literate men who appeared to have something in common with him. Some of them were the owners of fishing fleets – Simon, James, and John among them. Another was a doctor, another a civil servant who had first heard him speak in Capernaum.

'There must be twelve,' he said to them one day. 'There must be a zodiac.'

He was not careful in what he said. Many of his ideas were strange. Many of the things he talked about were unfamiliar to them. Some Pharisees thought he blasphemed.

One day he met a man he recognized as an Essene from the colony near Machaerus.

'John would speak with you,' said the Essene.

'Is John not dead yet?' he asked the man.

'He is confined at Peraea. I would think Herod is too frightened to kill him. He lets John walk about within the walls and gardens of the palace, lets him speak with his men, but John fears that Herod will find the courage soon to have him stoned or decapitated. He needs your help.'

'How can I help him? He is to die. There is no hope for him.'

The Essene looked uncomprehendingly into the mad eyes of the prophet.

'But, master, there is no one else who can help him.'

'I have done all that he wished me to do,' said the prophet. 'I have healed the sick and preached to the poor.'

'I did not know he wished this. Now he needs help, master. You could save his life.'

The prophet had drawn the Essene away from the crowd.

'His life cannot be saved.'

'But if it is not the unrighteous will prosper and the Kingdom of Heaven will not be restored.'

'His life cannot be saved.'

'Is it God's will?'

'If I am God, then it is God's will.'

Hopelessly, the Essene turned and began to walk away from the crowd.

John the Baptist would have to die. Glogauer had no wish to change history, only to strengthen it.

He moved on, with his following, through Galilee. He had selected his twelve educated men, and the rest who followed him were still primarily poor people. To them he offered their only hope of fortune. Many were those who had been ready to follow John against the Romans, but now John was imprisoned. Perhaps this man would lead them in revolt, to loot the riches of Jerusalem and Jericho and Caesarea. Tired and hungry, their eyes glazed by the burning sun, they followed the man in the white robe. They needed to hope and they found reasons for their hope. They saw him work greater miracles.

Once he preached to them from a boat, as was often his custom, and as he walked back to the shore through the shallows, it seemed to them that he walked over the water.

All through Galilee in the autumn they wandered, hearing from everyone the news of John's beheading. Despair at the Baptist's death turned to renewed hope in this new prophet who had known him.

In Caesarea they were driven from the city by Roman guards used to the wildmen with their prophecies who roamed the country.

They were banned from other cities as the prophet's fame grew. Not only the Roman authorities, but the Jewish ones as well seemed unwilling to tolerate the new prophet as they had tolerated John. The political climate was changing.

It became hard to find food. They lived on what they could find, hungering like starved animals.

He taught them how to pretend to eat and take their minds off their hunger.

Karl Glogauer, witch-doctor, psychiatrist, hypnotist, messiah.

Sometimes his conviction in his chosen role wavered and those that followed him would be disturbed when he contradicted himself. Often, now, they called him the name they had heard, Jesus the Nazarene. Most of the time he did not stop them from using the name, but at others he became angry and cried a peculiar, guttural name.

'Karl Glogauer! Karl Glogauer!'

And they said, Behold, he speaks with the voice of Adonai.

'Call me not by that name!' he would shout, and they would become disturbed and leave him by himself until his anger had subsided.

When the weather changed and the winter came, they went back to Capernaum, which had become a stronghold of his followers.

In Capernaum he waited the winter through, making prophecies.

Many of these prophecies concerned himself and the fate of those that followed him.

Then charged he his disciples that they should tell no man that he was Jesus the Christ. From that time forth began Jesus to shew unto his disciples, how that he must go unto Jerusalem and suffer many things of the elders and chief priests and scribes, and be killed, and be raised again the third day.

(Matthew 16:20–21)

They were watching television at her flat. Monica was eating an apple. It was between six and seven on a warm Sunday evening. Monica gestured at the screen with her half-eaten apple.

'Look at that nonsense,' she said. 'You can't honestly tell me it means anything to you.'

The programme was a religious one, about a pop-opera in a Hampstead Church. The opera told the story of the crucifixion.

'Pop-groups in the pulpit,' she said. 'What a come down.'

He didn't reply. The programme seemed obscene to him, in an obscure way. He couldn't argue with her.

'God's corpse is really beginning to rot now,' she jeered. 'Whew! The stink!'

'Turn it off, then,' he said quietly.

'What's the pop-group called? The Maggots?'

'Very funny. I'll turn it off, shall I?'

'No, I want to watch. It's funny.'

'Oh, turn it off!'

'Imitation of Christ!' she snorted. 'It's a bloody caricature.'

A negro singer, who was playing Christ and singing flat to a banal accompaniment, began to drone out lifeless lyrics about the brotherhood of man.

'If he sounded like that, no wonder they nailed him up,' said Monica.

He reached forward and switched the picture off.

'I was enjoying it.' She spoke with mock disappointment. 'It was a lovely swan-song.'

Later, she said with a trace of affection that worried him, 'You old fogey. What a pity. You could have been John Wesley or Calvin or someone. You can't be a messiah these days, not in your terms. There's nobody to listen.'

CHAPTER SIX

The prophet was living in the house of a man called Simon, though the prophet preferred to call him Peter. Simon was grateful to the prophet because he had cured his wife of a complaint which she had suffered from for some time. It had been a mysterious complaint, but the prophet had cured her almost effortlessly.

There were a great many strangers in Capernaum at that time; many of them coming to see the prophet. Simon warned the prophet that some were known agents of the Romans or the Pharisees. The Pharisees had not, on the whole, been antipathetic towards the prophet, though they distrusted the talk of miracles that they heard. However, the whole political atmosphere was disturbed and the Roman occupation troops, from Pilate, through his officers, down to the troops, were tense, expecting an outbreak but unable to see any tangible signs that one was coming.

Pilate himself hoped for trouble on a large scale. It would prove to Tiberius that the emperor had been too lenient with the Jews over the matter of the votive shields. Pilate would be vindicated and his power over the Jews increased. At present he was on bad terms with all the Tetrarchs of the provinces – particularly the unstable Herod Antipas who had seemed at one time his only supporter. Aside from the political situation, his own domestic situation was upset in that his neurotic wife was having her nightmares again and was demanding far more attention from him than he could afford to give her.

There might be a possibility, he thought, of provoking an incident, but he would have to be careful that Tiberius never learnt of it. This new prophet might provide a focus, but so far the man had done nothing against the laws of either the Jews or the Romans. There was no law that forbade a man to claim he was a messiah, as some said this one had done, and he was hardly inciting the people to revolt – rather the contrary.

Looking through the window of his chamber, with a view of the minarets and spires of Jerusalem, Pilate considered the information his spies had brought him.

Soon after the festival that the Romans called Saturnalia, the prophet and his followers left Capernaum again and began to travel through the country.

There were fewer miracles now that the hot weather had passed, but his prophecies were eagerly asked. He warned them of all the mistakes that would be made in the future, and of all the crimes that would be committed in his name.

Through Galiliee he wandered, and through Samaria, following the good Roman roads towards Jerusalem.

The time of the Passover was coming close now.

In Jerusalem, the Roman officials discussed the coming festival. It was always a time of the worst disturbances. There had been riots before during the Feast of the Passover, and doubtless there would be trouble of some kind this year, too.

Pilate spoke to the Pharisees, asking for their co-operation.

The Pharisees said they would do what they could but they could not help it if the people acted foolishly.

Scowling, Pilate dismissed them.

His agents brought him reports from all over the territory. Some of the reports mentioned the new prophet, but said that he was harmless.

Pilate thought privately that he might be harmless now, but if he reached Jerusalem during the Passover, he might not be so harmless.

Two weeks before the Feast of the Passover, the prophet reached the town of Bethany near Jerusalem. Some of his Galilean followers had friends in Bethany and these friends were more than willing to shelter the man they had heard of from other pilgrims on their way to Jerusalem and the Great Temple.

The reason they had come to Bethany was because the prophet had become disturbed at the number of the people following him.

'There are too many.' he had said to Simon. 'Too many, Peter.'

Glogauer's face was haggard now. His eyes were set deeper into their sockets and he said little.

Sometimes he would look around him vaguely, as if unsure where he was.

News came to the house in Bethany that Roman agents had been making enquiries about him. It did not seem to disturb him. On the contrary, he nodded thoughtfully, as if satisfied.

Once he walked with two of his followers across country to look at Jerusalem. The bright yellow walls of the city looked splendid in the afternoon light. The towers and tall buildings, many of them decorated in mosaic reds, blues and yellows, could be seen from several miles away.

The prophet turned back towards Bethany.

'When shall we go into Jerusalem?' one of his followers asked him.

'Not yet,' said Glogauer. His shoulders were hunched and he grasped his chest with his arms and hands as if cold.

Two days before the Feast of the Passover in Jerusalem, the prophet took his men towards the Mount of Olives and a suburb of Jerusalem that was built on its side and called Bethphage.

'Get me a donkey,' he told them. 'A colt. I must fulfil the

prophecy now.'

'Then all will know you are the Messiah,' said Andrew.

'Yes.'

Glogauer sighed. He felt afraid again, but this time it was not physical fear. It was the fear of an actor who was about to make his final, most dramatic scene and who was not sure he could do it well.

There was cold sweat on Glogauer's upper lip. He wiped it off.

In the poor light he peered at the men around him. He was still uncertain of some of their names. He was not interested in their names, particularly; only in their number. There were ten here. The other two were looking for the donkey.

They stood on the grassy slope of the Mount of Olives, looking towards Jerusalem and the great Temple which lay below. There was a light, warm breeze blowing.

'Judas?' said Glogauer enquiringly.

There was one called Judas.

'Yes, master,' he said. He was tall and good looking, with curly red hair and neurotic intelligent eyes. Glogauer believed he was an epileptic.

Glogauer looked thoughtfully at Judas Iscariot. 'I will want you to help me later,' he said, 'when we have entered Jerusalem.'

'How, master?'

'You must take a message to the Romans.'

'The Romans?' Iscariot looked troubled. 'Why?'

'It must be the Romans. It can't be the Jews – they would use a stake or an axe. I'll tell you more when the time comes.'

The sky was dark now, and the stars were out over the Mount of Olives. It had become cold. Glogauer shivered.

Rejoice greatly O daughter of Zion,
Shout, O daughter of Jerusalem:
Behold, thy King cometh unto thee!
He is just and having salvation;
Lowly and riding upon an ass,
And upon a colt, the foal of an ass.
(Zechariah 9:9)

'Osha'na! Osha'na! Osha'na!'

As Glogauer rode the donkey into the city, his followers ran ahead, throwing down palm branches. On both sides of the street were crowds, forewarned by the followers of his coming.

Now the new prophet could be seen to be fulfilling the prophecies of the ancient prophets and many believed that he had come to lead them against the Romans. Even now, possibly, he was on his way to Pilate's house to confront the procurator.

'Osha'na! Osha'na!'

Glogauer looked around distractedly. The back of the donkey, though softened by the coats of his followers, was uncomfortable. He swayed and clung to the beast's mane. He heard the words, but could not make them out clearly.

'Osha'na! Osha'na!'

It sounded like 'hosanna' at first, before he realized that they were shouting the Aramaic for 'Free us'.

'Free us! Free us!'

John had planned to rise in arms against the Romans this Passover. Many had expected to take part in the rebellion.

They believed that he was taking John's place as a rebel leader.

'No,' he muttered at them as he looked around at their expectant faces. 'No, I am the messiah. I cannot free you. I can't...'

They did not hear him above their own shouts.

Karl Glogauer entered Christ. Christ entered Jerusalem. The story was approaching its climax.

'Osha-na!'

It was not in the story. He could not help them.

Verily, verily, I say unto you, that one of you shall betray me. Then the disciples looked at one another, doubting of whom he spake. Now there was leaning on Jesus' bosom one of his disciples, whom Jesus loved. Simon Peter therefore beckoned to him, that he should ask who it should be of whom he spake. He then lying on Jesus' breast saith unto him, Lord, who is it? Jesus answered, He it is, to whom I shall give a sop, when I have dipped it. And when he had dipped the sop, he gave it to Judas Iscariot, the son of Simon. And after the sop Satan entered into him. Then said Jesus unto him, That thou doest, do quickly.

(John 13:20–27)

Judas Iscariot frowned with some uncertainty as he left the room and went out into the crowded street, making his way towards the governor's palace. Doubtless he was to perform a part in a plan to deceive the Romans and have the people rise up in Jesus' defence, but he thought the scheme foolhardy. The mood among the jostling men, women and children in the streets was tense. Many more Roman soldiers than usual patrolled the city.

Pilate was a stout man. His face was self-indulgent and his eyes were hard and shallow. He looked disdainfully at the Jew.

'We do not pay informers whose information is proved to be false,' he warned.

'I do not seek money, lord,' said Judas, feigning the ingratiating manner that the Romans seemed to expect of the Jews. 'I am a loyal subject of the Emperor.'

'Who is this rebel?'

'Jesus of Nazareth, lord. He entered the city today...'

'I know. I saw him. But I heard he preached of peace and obeying the law.'

'To deceive you, lord.'

Pilate frowned. It was likely. It smacked of the kind of deceit he had grown to anticipate in these soft-spoken people.

'Have you proof?'

'I am one of his lieutenants, lord. I will testify to his guilt.'

Pilate pursed his heavy lips. He could not afford to offend the Pharisees at this moment. They had given him enough trouble. Caiaphas, in particular, would be quick to cry 'injustice' if he arrested the man.

'He claims to be the rightful king of the Jews, the descendant of David,' said Judas, repeating what his master had told him to say.

'Does he?' Pilate looked thoughtfully out of the window.

'As for the Pharisees, lord ...'

'What of them?'

'The Pharisees distrust him. They would see him dead. He speaks against them.'

Pilate nodded. His eyes were hooded as he considered this information. The Pharisees might hate the madman, but they would be quick to make political capital out of his arrest.

'The Pharisees want him arrested,' Judas continued. 'The people flock to listen to the prophet and today many of them rioted in the Temple in his name.'

'Is this true?'

'It is true, lord.' It was true. Some half a dozen people had attacked the money-changers in the Temple and tried to rob them. When they had been arrested, they had said they had been carrying out the will of the Nazarene.

'I cannot make the arrest,' Pilate said musingly. The situation in Jerusalem was already dangerous, but if they were to arrest this 'king', they might find that they precipitated a revolt. Tiberius would blame him, not the Jews. The Pharisees must be won over. They must make the arrest. 'Wait here,' he said to Judas, 'I will send a message to Caiaphas.'

And they came to a place which was named Gethsemane: and he saith to his disciples, Sit ye here, while I shall pray. And he taketh with him Peter and James and John, and began to be sore amazed, and to be very heavy; and saith unto them, My soul is exceeding sorrowful unto death: tarry ye here, and watch.

(Mark 14:32–4)

Glogauer could see the mob approaching now. For the first time since Nazareth he felt physically weak and exhausted. They were going to kill him. He had to die; he accepted that, but he was afraid of the pain that was to come. He sat down on the ground of the hillside, watching the torches as they came closer.

'The ideal of martyrdom only ever existed in the minds of a few ascetics,' Monica had said. 'Otherwise it was morbid masochism, an easy way to forgo ordinary responsibility, a method of keeping repressed people under control...'

'It isn't as simple as that...'

'It is, Karl.'

He could show Monica now. His regret was that she was unlikely ever to know. He had meant to write everything down and put it into the time machine and hope that it would be recovered. It was strange. He was not a religious man in the usual sense. He was an agnostic. It was not conviction that had led him to defend religion against Monica's cynical contempt for it; it was rather *lack* of conviction in the ideal in which she had set her own faith, the ideal of science as a solver of all problems. He could not share her faith and there was nothing else but religion, though he could not believe in the kind of God of Christianity. The God seen as a mystical force of the mysteries of Christianity and other great religions had not been personal enough for him. His rational mind had told him that God did not exist in any personal form. His unconscious had told him that faith in science was not enough.

'Science is basically opposed to religion,' Monica had once said harshly. *No matter how many Jesuits get together and rationalize their views of science, the fact remains that religion cannot accept the fundamental attitudes of science and it is implicit to science to attack the fundamental principles of religion. The only area in which there is no difference and need be no war is in the ultimate assumption. One may or may not assume there is a supernatural being called God. But as soon as one begins to defend one's assumption, there must be strife.'*

'You're talking about organized religion . . .'

'I'm talking about religion as opposed to a belief. Who needs the ritual of religion when we have the far superior ritual of science to replace it? Religion is a reasonable substitute for knowledge. But there is no longer any need for substitutes, Karl. Science offers a sounder basis on which to formulate systems of thought and ethics. We don't need the carrot of heaven and the big stick of hell any more when science can show the consequences of actions and men can judge easily for themselves whether those actions are right or wrong.'

'I can't accept it.'

'That's because you're sick. I'm sick, too, but at least I can see the promise of health.'

'I can only see the threat of death . . .'

As they had agreed, Judas kissed him on the cheek and the mixed force of Temple guards and Roman soldiers surrounded him.

To the Romans he said, with some difficulty, 'I am the King of the Jews.' To the Pharisees' servants he said: 'I am the messiah who has come to destroy your masters.' Now he was committed, and the final ritual was to begin.

CHAPTER SEVEN

It was an untidy trial, an arbitrary mixture of Roman and Jewish law which did not altogether satisfy anyone. The object was accomplished after several conferences between Pontius Pilate and Caiaphas and three attempts to bend and merge their separate legal systems in order to fit the expediencies of the situation. Both needed a scapegoat for their different purposes and so at last the result was achieved and the madman convicted, on the one hand of rebellion against Rome and on the other of heresy.

A peculiar feature of the trial was that the witnesses were all followers of the man and yet had seemed eager to see him convicted.

The Pharisees agreed that the Roman method of execution would fit the time and the situation best in this case and it was decided to crucify him. The man had prestige, however, so that it would be necessary to use some of the tried Roman methods of humiliation in order to make him into a pathetic and ludicrous figure in the eyes of the pilgrims. Pilate assured the Pharisees that he would see to it, but he made sure that they signed documents that gave their approval to his actions.

> *And the soldiers led him away into the hall, called Praetorium; and they called together the whole band. And they clothed him with purple, and plaited a crown of thorns, and put it about his head, And began to salute him, Hail, King of the Jews! And they smote him on the head with a reed, and did spit upon him, and bowing their knees worshipped him. And when they had mocked him, they took off the purple from him, and put his own clothes on him, and led him out to crucify him.*
>
> (Mark 15:16–20)

His brain was clouded now, by pain and by the ritual of humiliation; by his having completely given himself up to his role.

He was too weak to bear the heavy wooden cross and he walked behind it as it was dragged towards Golgotha by a Cyrenian whom the Romans had press-ganged for the purpose.

As he staggered through the crowded, silent streets, watched by those who had thought he would lead them against the Roman overlords, his eyes filled with tears so that his sight was blurred and he occasionally staggered off the road and was nudged back on to it by one of the Roman guards.

'You are too emotional, Karl. Why don't you use that brain of yours and pull yourself together . . .'

He remembered the words, but it was difficult to remember who had said them or who Karl was.

The road that led up the side of the hill was stony and he slipped sometimes, remembering another hill he had climbed long ago. It seemed to him that he had been a child, but the memory merged with others and it was impossible to tell.

He was breathing heavily and with some difficulty. The pain of the thorns in his head was barely felt, but his whole body seemed to throb in unison with his heartbeat. It was like a drum.

It was evening. The sun was setting. He fell on his face, cutting his head on a sharp stone, just as he reached the top of the hill. He fainted.

And they brought him unto the place Golgotha, which is being interpreted, The place of the skull. And they gave him to drink wine mingled with myrrh: but he received it not.

(Mark 15:22–3)

He knocked the cup aside. The soldier shrugged and reached out for one of his arms. Another soldier already held the other arm.

As he recovered consciousness Glogauer began to tremble violently. He felt the pain intensely as the ropes bit into the flesh of his wrists and ankles. He struggled.

He felt something cold placed against his palm. Although it only covered a small area in the centre of his hand it seemed very heavy. He heard a sound that also was in rhythm with his heartbeats. He turned his head to look at the hand.

The large iron peg was being driven into his hand by a soldier swinging a mallet as he lay on the cross which was at this moment horizontal on the ground. He watched, wondering why there was no pain. The soldier swung the mallet higher as the peg met the resistance of the wood. Twice he missed the peg and struck Glogauer's fingers.

Glogauer looked to the other side and saw that the second soldier was also hammering in a peg. Evidently he missed the peg a great many times because the fingers of the hand were bloody and crushed.

The first soldier finished hammering in his peg and turned his attention to the feet. Glogauer felt the iron slide through his flesh, heard it hammered home.

Using a pulley, they began to haul the cross into a vertical position. Glogauer noticed that he was alone. There were no others being crucified that day.

He got a clear view of the lights of Jersualem below him. There was still a little light in the sky but not much. Soon it would be completely dark. There was a small crowd looking on. One of the women reminded him of Monica. He called to her.

'Monica?'

But his voice was cracked and the word was a whisper. The woman did not look up.

He felt his body dragging at the nails which supported it. He thought he felt a twinge of pain in his left hand. He seemed to be bleeding very heavily.

It was odd, he reflected, that it should be him hanging here. He supposed that it was the event he had originally come to witness. There was little doubt, really. Everything had gone perfectly.

The pain in his left hand increased.

He glanced down at the Roman guards who were playing dice at the foot of his cross. They seemed absorbed in their game. He could not see the markings of the dice from this distance.

He sighed. The movement of his chest seemed to throw extra strain on his hands. The pain was quite bad now. He winced and tried somewhow to ease himself back against the wood.

The pain began to spread through his body. He gritted his teeth. It was dreadful. He gasped and shouted. He writhed.

There was no longer any light in the sky. Heavy clouds obscured stars and moon.

From below came whispered voices.

'Let me down,' he called. 'Oh, please let me down!'

The pain filled him. He slumped forward, but nobody released him.

A little while later he raised his head. The movement caused a return of the agony and again he began to writhe on the cross.

'Let me down. Please. Please stop it!'

Every part of his flesh, every muscle and tendon and bone of him, was filled with an almost impossible degree of pain.

He knew he would not survive until the next day as he had thought he might. He had not realized the extent of his pain.

And at the ninth hour Jesus cried with a loud voice, saying,

'Eloi, Eloi, lama sabachthani?' which is, being interpreted, My God, my God, why hast thou forsaken me?

(Mark 15:34)

Glogauer coughed. It was a dry, barely heard sound. The soldiers below the cross heard it because the night was now so quiet.

'It's funny,' one said. 'Yesterday they were worshipping him. Today they seemed to want us to kill him – even the ones who were closest to him.'

'I'll be glad when we get out of this country,' said another.

He heard Monica's voice again. "It's weakness and fear, Karl, that's driven you to this. Martyrdom is a conceit. Can't you see that?'

Weakness and fear.

He coughed once more and the pain returned, but it was duller now.

Just before he died he began to talk again, muttering the words until his breath was gone. 'It's a lie. It's a lie. It's a lie.'

Later, after his body was stolen by the servants of doctors who believed it to have special properties, there were rumours that he had not died. But the corpse was already rotting in the doctors' dissecting rooms and would soon be destroyed.

GOOD-BYE, MIRANDA

Good-bye, Miranda.

Good-bye, Miranda.

Miranda.

He swerved and swooped over the grey water like a seabird. He was quite mad.

Good-bye, Miranda.

His crying laugh was ugly against the sounds of the sea. It held far too much pain for any listeners to sympathize with it. They could only react against that sound, try to stop it, quickly. But they couldn't catch him. Nicholas could fly.

Miranda!

'I wish I had a gun, Miranda.'

'Would you kill him, father?'

'Sure I would. Kill him dead. Why's he do it?'

'He's mad, father. If I got you a gun, would you kill him?'

'Sure I would, dead. I can't stand it. He's tormenting us deliberate.'

'I loved him.'

'I know you did – once. But that don't give him the excuse to come wailing round here. Just like a banshee. Just like one.'

'It's love, father – love turned to madness. He *ought* to be shot. It's what he wants, I think.'

'It's what I want, anyhow.'

They stayed in the little house on the headland. They wouldn't go out. But he'd been outside for two days and nights, now. The flying madman. Well, he shouldn't have told them about that – levitation – should've kept it to himself. A man needn't know. But if he does, then he's got to do something about it. He couldn't have his daugher marrying – a spook.

Now look what had happened. He'd found them, at last. Miranda had said he would.

By God, if only he had a gun . . .

Please come out and say good-bye to me, Miranda.

He was on the roof again.

It's only me – Nicholas.

By the chimney, shouting in that high voice, just like a bird's.

Say good-bye to me, Miranda.

She was covering her ears. Her face bunched up in the terrible pain his voice made on her nerves. It was physical pain. 'Stop him, father!'

'How can I stop him? If I had a gun I'd shoot him dead.'

'We've got to get a gun.'

'Where? Where can we get one?'

'You'll have to go to the village.'

'Not with him out there.'

Oh, Miranda. Just good-bye.

'Good-bye, good-bye, good-bye! Go away, Nicholas! Go *away*! Please!'

'He's doing it deliberate. My God, he'll have us mad, too. I'll go down to the village tomorrow. I'll risk it. Three days. My God!'

Miranda!

'Tomorrow,' he said. 'Tomorrow, I'll definitely go.'

'You said that yesterday.'

'Well, I'll go tomorrow. Doesn't he sleep?'

Miranda! Good-bye.

She leapt at her father, her pale hands tearing. 'Go, father. Get the gun! The gun! The gun!'

'Tomorrow.' He struggled with her. 'Stop that. I said I'd go tomorrow and I will.' His yellow fingers gripped her. 'Stop that, now, Miranda!'

'The *gun*!'

'Go away, Nicholas!'

Her breathing was a thin noise. She was dirty, her face was lined and the knife was still in her hand. Her father's blood dripped on to her father's corpse.

Just good-bye, Miranda. That's all. I love you.

Her thin body shuddered.

She walked towards the door, each step carefully made. She reached for the bolt and the brown sleeve fell down her bruised arm. She pulled back the bolt.

'Go away, Nicholas!'

She heard his voice among the torn clouds. *Miranda!*

The air was sharp, as sharp as his voice.

She looked up, over the roof of the house and glimpsed his mad body darting, gliding. She heard the passing of his body above her and saw it wheeling over the sea, heard the voice, shrill, agonized: *Good-bye, Miranda.* She became aware of the heart pushing at her flesh, beneath her breast. She gripped the knife.

Miranda!

'Oh . . .' she said as the knife pierced her and she began to fall, first against the swinging door, then back, dropping with a flat sound on the stones of the floor.

When he came back, he saw that the light was swirling around outside the door, released from the house and dissipating into the night. He landed beside the door but was too physically weak to walk so had to glide into the house and see the corpses.

He was puzzled. His dark, thin, ravaged face moved with the effort of thought, but thought was now beyond him.

Miranda?

He shook his head slowly, but it was no good.

His body moved backwards out of the door, a foot above the ground.

Good-bye, Miranda.

He flew away, but he was still calling, and strangely there was no sorrow in the cry.

FLUX

Max File leaned forward, addressing an impatient question towards the driving compartment. 'How long now before we get there?'

Then he remembered that this car had no driver. Usually, as Marshall-in-Chief of the European Defensive Nuclear Striking Force, he allowed himself the luxury of a chauffeur; but today his destination was secret and known not even to himself.

The plan of his route lay safely locked away in the computer of the car's automatic controller.

He settled back in his seat, deciding that it was useless to fret.

The car left the Main Way about half a mile before it met up with the central traffic circuit which flung vehicles and goods into the surrounding urban system like a gigantic whirling wheel. The car was making for the older parts of the city, nearest the ground. For this, File was grateful, though he did not overtly admit it to himself. Above him, the horizon-wide drone and vibrating murmur of this engineer's paradise still went on, but at least it was more diffuse. The noise was just as great, but more chaotic, and therefore more pleasing to File's ear. Twice the car was forced to pause before dense streams of pedestrians issuing from public pressure train stations, faces set and sweating as they battled their way to work.

File sat impassively through the delay, though already he was late for the meeting. What did it mean, he wondered, this Gargantua which sat perpetually bellowing athwart the whole continent? It never slept; it never ceased proudly to roar out its own power. And however benevolent it was towards its hundreds of millions of inhabitants, there was no denying that they were, every one, its slaves.

How had it arisen, what would become of it? It was already so overgrown internally that only with difficulty human beings found themselves room to live in it. If it were seen from out in space, he thought, no human beings would be visible; it would seem to be only a fast-moving machine of marvellous power but no purpose.

Max File did not have much faith in the European Economic Community's ability to prolong its life infinitely. It had grown swiftly, but it had grown by itself, without the benefit of proper human design. Already, he thought, he could detect the seeds of inevitable collapse.

Patiently, the car eased forward through the crowd, found an unobstructed lane and then continued on its complicated route. Eventually it made its way through a tangle of signs, directions and cross-overs, before stopping in front of a small ten-storey building bearing a grim but solid stamp of authority.

There were guards at the entrance, betokening the gravity of the emergency. File was escorted to a suite on the fifth floor. Here, he was ushered into a windowless chamber with panelled wood walls and a steady, quiet illumination. At the oval table, the Government of the European Economic Community had already convened and was waiting silently for his arrival. The ministers looked up as he entered.

They made an oddly serene and formal group, with their uniformly dark conservative dress and the white note-paper lying unmarked in neat squares before them. An air of careful constraint prevailed in the room. Most of the ministers gave File only distant nods as he entered and then cast their eyes primly downward as before. File returned the nods. He was acquainted with them all, but not closely. For some reason they always tended to keep their distance from him, in spite of the high position he held – and for which he seemed to have been destined since childhood.

Only Prime Minister Strasser rose to welcome him.

'Please be seated, File,' he said. File shook the old man's proferred hand, then made his way to his place. Strasser began to speak at once, clearly intending to make the meeting brief and to the point.

'As we all know,' he began, 'the situation in Europe has reached the verge of civil war. However, most of us also know that we are not here today to discuss a course of action – I speak now for your benefit, File. We are here to understand our position, and to propose a mission.'

Strasser sat down and nodded perfunctorily to the man on his left. Standon, pale and bony, inclined his head towards File and spoke.

'When we first sat down to deal with this problem, we

thought it differed from no other crisis in history – that we would first consider the aims and intention of the quarrelling economic and political factions, decide which to back and which to fight. It was not long before we discovered our error.

'First, we realized that Europe is only a political entity and not a national entity, obviating the most obvious basis for action. Then we tried to comprehend the entire system which we think of as Europe – and failed. As an industrial economy, Europe passes comprehension!'

He paused, and a strange emotion seemed to well just beneath the surface of his face. He moved his body uneasily, then continued in a stronger tone.

'We are the first government in history which is aware, and will admit, that it does not know how to control events. The continent in our charge has become the most massive, complex, high-pressured phenomenon ever to appear on the face of this planet. We no more know how to control it than we know how to control the mechanism governing the growth of an actual living organism. Some of us are of the opinion that European industry has in fact become a living organism – but one without the sanity and certainty of proper development that a natural organism has. It began haphazardly, and then followed its own laws. There is one of us –' he indicated stern Brown-Gothe across the table – 'who equates it with a cancer.'

File mused on the similarity of the minister's conclusions to his own thoughts of only a few minutes before.

'Europe suffers from compression,' Standon continued. 'Everything is so pressurized, energies and processes abut so solidly on one another, that the whole system has massed together in a solid plenum. Politically speaking, there just isn't room to move around. Consequently, we are unable to apprehend the course of events either by computation or by common sense, and we are unable to say what will result from any given action. In short, we are in complete ignorance of the future, whether we participate in it or not.'

File looked up and down the table. Most of the ministers still gazed passively at their notepads. One or two, with Strasser and Standon, were looking at him expectantly.

'I had been coming to the same conclusion myself,' he said. 'But you must have decided upon something.'

'No,' said Standon forcefully. 'This is the essence of the matter. If things were that clear-cut there would not be this problem – we should simply choose a side. But there are not two factions – there are three or four, with others in the background. The very idea of what is best loses meaning when we do not know what is going to happen. Logically, destruction of the community is the only criterion of what is undesirable, but even then, who knows? Perhaps we have grown so monstrous that there is no possibility of our further existence. There are no ideals to guide us. And in any case, there is no longer deliberate direction as far as Europe is concerned.'

Standon took his eyes off File and seemed to withdraw for a moment. 'I might add,' he said, 'that after having had several weeks to think about it, we are of the opinion that this has always been the case in political affairs: only the fact that there was space to move around in gave the statesmen of the past the illusion that they were free to determine events. Now there is no empty space, the illusion has vanished and we are aware of our helplessness. At the same time, everything is much more frightening.'

He shrugged. 'For instance, Europe, because of its massiveness, could absorb a large number of nuclear fusion explosions and still keep functioning. I need hardly add that at the present time such weapons are available to any large-scale corporation. We even think there are some small-yield bombs in the hands of minority groups.'

File reflected as calmly as he could. Suddenly the crisis had slid over the edge of practical considerations into the realm of philosophy. It sounded absurd, but there was no denying the fact.

He appreciated the caution of those very self-composed men. Like them, he had a fear of tyranny, but history provided many warnings against hasty preventive measures. It was to avert tyranny that the conspirators murdered Caesar, yet within hours the consequences of their foolish deed had plunged the state into a reign of terror even worse than anything they had imagined. The ministers were right: there was no such thing as free will, and a state was manageable only if it was uncomplicated enough not to go off the rails in any case.

He said: 'I presume everything has been done to try to analyse events? Cybernetics . . .?'

Standon gave him a tolerant smile. 'Everything has been done.'

As if this were a cue, a third man spoke. Appeltoft, whose

special province was science and technology, was younger than the others and somewhat more emotional. He looked up to address File.

'Our only hope lies in discovering how events are organized in time – this might sound highly speculative for such a serious and practical matter, but this is what things have come to. In order to take effective action in the present, we must first know the future. This is the mission we have in mind for you. The Research Complex at Geneva has found a way to deposit a man some years in the future and bring him back. You will be sent ten years forward to find out what will happen and how it will come about. You will then return, report your findings to us, and we will use this information to guide our actions, and also – scientifically – to analyse the laws governing the sequence of time. This is how we hope to formulate a method of human government for use by future ages, and, perhaps, remove the random element from human affairs.'

File was impressed by the striking, unconventional method the Cabinet had adopted to resolve its dilemma.

'You leave immediately,' Appeltoft told him, breaking in on his thoughts. 'After this conference, you and I will fly to Geneva where the technicians have the apparatus in readiness.' A hint of bitterness came into his voice. 'I had wished to go myself, but . . .' he shrugged and made a vague, disgusted gesture which took in the rest of the Cabinet.

'That's a point,' File said. 'Why have you chosen me?'

The ministers looked at one another shiftily. Strasser spoke up.

'The reason lies in your education, Max,' he said diffidently. 'The difficulties facing us now were beginning to show themselves over a generation ago. The government of the time decided to bring up a small number of children according to a new system of education. The idea was to develop people capable of comprehending in detail the massiveness of modern civilization, by means of forced learning in every subject. The experiment failed. All your schoolfellows lost their sanity. You survived, but did not turn into the product we had hoped for. To prevent any later derangement of your mind, a large part of the information which had been pressurized into it was removed by hypnotic means. The result is yourself as you are – a super-dilettante, with an intense curiosity and a gift for management. We gave you the post you now hold, and forgot about you. Now you are ideal for our purpose.'

Inwardly, File underwent a jolt: even more so because the account agreed well with his own suspicions concerning his origins. He pulled himself together before he could become introspective.

'I was the only one to make it, eh? I wonder why.'

Standon regarded File steadily in the dim light. Once again that strange layer of emotion seemed to stir in him, lying somewhere below his features, but not affecting the muscles or skin.

'Because of your determination, Mr File. Because whatever happens, somehow, you have the capacity to find a way out.'

File left the building even more aware of his speculations than before. Appeltoft came with him, and the car whined smoothly towards the nearest air centre.

He had a peg to hang his thoughts on now. The sequence of time ... Yes, there was no doubt that the explanation of the titanic phenomena through which he was being driven, lay in the sequence of time.

Looking around him, he saw how literally true were the statements just given him by the ministers.

After the formation of the Economic Community, into which all the European countries were finally joined, the continent's capacity had accelerated fantastically. Economic development had soared so high that eventually it became necessary to buttress up the whole structure from underneath. Stage by stage, the buttresses had become more massive, until the community was tied to the ground, a rigid unchangeable monster, humming and roaring with energy.

Even the airy architectural promise of the previous century had not materialized. The constructions wheeling past the car had an appearance of Wagnerian heaviness, blocking out the sunlight.

He turned to Appeltoft. 'So in an hour I'll be ten years in the future. Ridiculous statement!'

Appeltoft laughed, as though to show he appreciated the paradox.

'But tell me,' File continued, 'are you really so ignorant about time's nature, and yet you can effect travel in it?'

'We are not so ignorant about its nature, as about its structure and organization,' Appeltoft told him. 'The equations which enable us to transmit through time give no clue to that – in fact they say that time has no sequence at all, which can hardly be possible.'

Appeltoft paused. His manner towards File gave the latter cause to think that the scientist still resented not being allowed to be the first time traveller, though he was trying to hide it. File didn't blame him. When a man has worked fanatically for something, it must be a blow to see a complete stranger take over the fruits of it.

'There are two theories extant,' Appeltoft eventually went on. 'The first, and the one I favour, is the common-sense view – past, present, future, proceeding in an unending line and each event having a definite position on the line. Unfortunately the idea has not lent itself to any mathematical formulation.

'The other idea, which some of my co-workers hold, goes like this: that time isn't really a forward-moving flow at all. It exists as a constant: all things are actually happening at once, but human beings haven't got the built-in perceptions to see it as such. Imagine a circular stage with a sequence of events going on round it, representing, say, periods in one man's life. In that case they would be played by different actors, but in the actuality of time the same man plays all parts. According to this, an alteration in one scene has an effect on all subsequent scenes all the way round back to the beginning.'

'So that time is cyclic – what you do in the future may influence your future past, as it were?'

'If the theory is correct. Some formulations have been derived, but they don't work very well. All we really know, is that we can deposit you into the future and probably bring you back.'

'Probably! You've had failures?'

'Thirty-three per cent of our test animals don't return,' Appeltoft said blithely.

Once they were at the air centre, it took them less than an hour to reach the Geneva Research Complex. From the air receptor on the roof, Appeltoft conducted him nearly half a mile down to the underground laboratories. Finally, he pulled an old-fashioned key-chain from his pocket, attached to which was a little radio-key. As he pressed the stud a door swung open a few yards ahead.

They entered a blue-painted chamber whose walls were lined with what looked like computer programme inlets. A number of white-robed technicians sat about, waiting.

Occupying the centre of the room was a chair, mounted on a pedestal. A swivel arm held a small box with instrument dials on the external surfaces; but the most notable feature was the three translucent rods which seemed to ray out from just behind the chair, one going straight up, and the other two at right angles one on either side.

The floor was covered with trestles supporting a network of helices and semi-conductor electron channels, radiating out from the chair like a spider's web. File found himself trying to interpret the set-up in the pseudo-scientific jargon which was his way of understanding contemporary technology. Electrons ... indeterminacy ... what would the three rods be for?

'This is the time transmission apparatus,' Appeltoft told him without preamble.

'The actual apparatus itself will remain here in the present time: only that chair, with you sitting in it, will make the time transference itself.'

'So you will control everything from here?'

'Not exactly. It will be a "powered flight", so to speak, and you will carry the controls. But the power unit will remain here. We might be able to do something if the mission goes wrong, perhaps not. We probably won't even know.

'The three rods accompanying the chair represent the three spatial dimensions. As these rotate out of true space, time-motion will begin.'

Stepping carefully across the trestles, they walked nearer to the chair. Appeltoft explained the controls and instruments. 'This is your speed gauge – you've no way of controlling that, it's all automatic. This switch here is "stop" and "start" – it's marked, you'll notice. And this one gives the point in time you occupy, in years, days, hours, and seconds. Everything else is programmed for you. As you see, it reads nil now. When you arrive it will read ten years.'

'Point in time, eh?' File mused. 'That could have two meanings according to what you've just told me.'

Appeltoft nodded. 'You're astute. Pragmatically, my own view of straight line time is closest to the operation of the time transmitter. It's the easiest to grasp, anyway.'

File studied the apparatus for nearly a minute without speaking. The silence dragged on. Though he wasn't aware of it, strain was growing.

'Well, don't just stand there,' Appeltoft snapped with sudden ferocity. 'Get on the damned thing! We haven't got all day!'

File gave him a look of surprised reproof.

Appeltoft sagged. 'Sorry. If you knew – how jealous I am of you. To be the first man with a chance to discover the secret of time! It's the secret of the universe itself.'

Well, File thought to himself, as he watched the young minister's lean, intense face, *if I had his determination I might have been a scientist and made discoveries for myself, instead of being a jacked-up dilettante*. 'A dilettante,' he muttered aloud.

'Eh?' Appeltoft said. 'Well, come on, let's get it done.'

File climbed into the seat built into the back of the chair, camera lenses peered over his shoulders. 'You know what to look for?' Appeltoft asked finally.

'As much as anybody. Besides – I want to go as much as you do.'

'All right then. Capacity's built up. Press the switch to "start". It will automatically revert to "stop" at the end of the journey.'

File obeyed. At first, nothing happened. Then he got the impression that the translucent rods, which he could see out of the corners of his eyes, were rotating clockwise, though they didn't seem to change their positions. At the same time, the room appeared to spin in the opposite direction – again, it was movement without change of position.

The effect was entirely like having drunk too much, and File felt dizzy. He pulled his eyes to the speed gauge. One minute per minute – marking time! One and a half, two . . .

With a weird flickering effect the laboratory vanished. He was in a neutral grey fog, left only with sensation.

The first sensation was that he was taking part in the rotating movement – being steadily canted to the left. As his angle to the vertical increased, the second sensation increased; a rushing momentum, a gathering speed towards a nameless destination.

000001.146.15.0073 – the numbers slipped into place, swiftly towards the right-hand side, slowly towards the left. 000002–3–4–5–6–7–

Then the nausea returned, the feeling of being spun round – the other way, now. Lights dazzled his eyes.

000010.000.00.0000.

When he grew used to it, the light was really dim. He was

still in the laboratory, but it was deserted, illuminated by emergency lights glowing weakly in the ceiling. It was not in ruins, and there was no sign of violence, but the place had obviously been empty for some time.

Climbing down from the chair, he went to the door, used the radio key which Appeltoft had given him, went through and closed it behind him. He walked along the corridor and through the other departments.

The whole complex shouldn't be deserted after only ten years ... something drastic must have happened.

He frowned, annoyed at himself. Of course it had. That was why he was here.

The high-level streets of Geneva were equally deserted. He could see the tops of mountains in the distance, poking between metallic roadways. The drone of the city was missing. There was some noise to be heard, but it was muted and irregular.

As he mounted an inter-level ramp he saw one or two figures, mostly alone. He had never seen so few people. Perhaps the quickest way to find out what was going on would be to locate the library and read up some recent history. It might give a clue, anyway.

He reached the building which pushed up through several layers of deserted street. A huge black sign hung over the entrance. It said:

MEN ONLY

Puzzled, File entered the cool half-light and approached the wary young man at the Inquiry Desk.

'Excuse me,' he said and jumped as the man produced a squat gun from under the counter and levelled it at him.

'What do you want?'

'I've come to consult recent texts dealing with the development of Europe in the last ten years,' File said.

The young man grinned with his thin lips. The gun held steady, he said: 'Development?'

'I'm a serious student – all I want to do is look up some information.'

The young man put away the gun and with one hand pressed the buttons of an index system. He took two cards out and handed them to File.

'Fifth floor, room 543. Here's the key. Lock the door behind you. Last week a gang of women broke through the barricades and tried to burn us down. They like their meat pre-cooked, eh?'

File frowned at him, but said nothing. He went to the elevator. The young man called: 'For a student you don't know much about this library. The elevator hasn't worked for four years. The women control all the main power sources these days.'

Still in a quandary, File walked up to the fifth floor, found the room he wanted, unlocked the door, entered and locked it behind him.

Seating himself before the viewer, he pressed the appropriate buttons on the panel before him and the pages started to appear on the screen.

Hmmm ... Let's see ... Investigations of Dalmeny Foundation members. Paper VII: PARTIAL RESULTS OF THE BAVARIAN EXPERIMENT ...

– Civil war imminent, the Council temporaily averted it by promising that thorough research would be made into every claim for a solution to the problems of over-compression. This, as we know now, was a stonewalling action since they later admitted they had been incapable of predicting the outcome of any trend. The faction, one of the most powerful, headed by the late Stefan Untermeyer, demanded that they be allowed to conduct a controlled experiment.

– Unable to stall any longer, the Council reluctantly agreed, and a large part of Bavaria was set aside so that the plans of the Untermeyer faction could be implemented. This plan necessitated sexual segregation. Men and women were separated and each given an intensive psycho-conditioning to hate the opposite sex. Next, acts were passed making contact with the opposite sex punishable by death. This act had to be enforced frequently, although not as frequently as originally had been thought. Ironically, Untermeyer was one of the first to be punished under the act.

– It is difficult these days, to make a clear assessment of the results of this experiment (which so quickly got out of hand and resulted in the literal war between the sexes, which now exists with cannibalism so prevalent, each sex regarding it as lawful to eat a member of the other) but it is obvious that measures for reassimilation have so far met with little success and that, since this creed has now spread through Germany,

Scandinavia, and elsewhere, an incredible depletion of life in Northern Europe is likely. In the long run, of course, repopulation will result as the roving hordes from France and Spain press northwards. Europe, having collapsed, is ready for conquest and when the squabblings of America and the United East are ended, either by bloodshed or peaceful negotiation, Europe's only salvation may be in coming under the sway of one of these powers. However, as we know, both these powers have similar problems to those of Europe in its last days of sanity.

File pursed his lips, consulted the other card and pressed a fresh series of buttons.

– Nobody could have predicted this. But by the look of it there's more to come. Let's see what this is: FINDINGS OF THE VINER COMMITTEE FOR THE INVESTIGATION OF SOCIAL DISINTEGRATION IN SOUTHERN EUROPE . . .

– The terms of reference of the Committee were as follows: To investigate the disintegration of the pre-experimental European society in southern Europe and to suggest measures for reorganizing the society into an operating whole.

– Briefly, as is generally known, the European Council gave permission for the Population Phasing Group to conduct an experiment in Greece. The Group, using the principles of suspended animation discovered a few years earlier by Batchovski, instituted total birth-control and placed three-quarters of the population of Greece into suspended animation, the other quarter being thought sufficient to run public and social services and so on, reasoning, quite rationally it seemed, that in this way further population explosion would be averted, less overcrowding would result and the pace of our society could be relaxed. After a given time, the first quarter would go into suspended animation and be replaced by the next quarter and so on. This phasing process did seem to be the most reasonable solution to the Problem of Europe, as it was called.

– However, in ridding the population of claustrophobia, the system produced an effect of extreme agoraphobia. The people, being used to living close together, became restless, and the tension which had preceded the introduction of the PPG Experiment, was turned into new channels. Mobs, exhibiting signs of extreme neurosis, completely insensate and deaf to all reason, attacked what were called the S.A. Vaults and demanded the release of their relatives and friends. The authorities attempted to argue with them but, in the turmoil which followed, were either killed or forced to flee. Unable to operate the machines keeping the rest of the population in suspended animation, the mobs destroyed them, killing the people they had intended to reawaken.

– When the Committee reached Southern Europe, they found a declining society. Little attempt had been made to retrieve the situation, people were living in the vast depopulated conurbations in little groups, fighting off the influx of roaming bands from France, Spain, and Italy, where earlier a religious fanatic had, quite unexpectedly, started a jehad against the automated, but workable, society. This 'back to nature' movement snowballed. Power installations were destroyed and millions of tons of earth were imported from Africa to spread over the ruins. In the chaos which ensued people fought and squabbled over what little food could be grown in the unproductive earth where it had been imported and in the Holiday Spaces. Britain, already suffering from the effects of this breakdown and unable to obtain sufficient supplies to feed its own population properly, had begun sending aid but had been forced to give up this measure and look to its own problems – the sudden spread of an unknown disease, similar to typhus, which was found to have come from Yugoslav refugees who had themselves suffered badly from the introduction of a synthetic food product which contained the germs. By the time we reached Southern Europe, the social services all over the continent had disintegrated and only the Dalmeny Foundation (which had commissioned us) and half a dozen less well-organized groups were managing to maintain any kind of academic activity . . .

As File read on through the depressing texts, he felt the blood leave his face. At length he had checked and rechecked the documents; he sat back and contemplated.

The blundering nature of the experiments appalled him. Nothing could be a better confirmation of what he had been told at the Cabinet Meeting, and it made him doubt, now, that anything at all could be done to avert the calamity. If men were so blind and foolish, could even Appeltoft's incisive mind save them? Even supposing he succeeded in making a clear, workable analysis of the science of events from the information File had obtained . . .

That part of it was out of his hands, he realized, and perhaps Appeltoft's confidence stood for something. Impatiently he rushed back to the laboratory, mounted the chair of the time machine, and pressed the switch to 'start'. 000009.000. 0000003 ...

Soon there was a grey mist surrounding him as before. Rotation and momentum began to impress themselves on his senses.

Then his gauges jigged and danced, clicked and tumbled insanely, 009000.100.02.0000 – 000175.000.03.0800 – 630946.020.44.1125.

Something had gone wrong. Desperately he tried to stop the machine and inspect the controls. Every dial registered noughts now.

But the laboratory was gone. He was surrounded by darkness.

He was in limbo.

–000000.000.00.0000.

File did not know how long he sped through the emptiness. Gradually, the mistiness began to return, then, after what seemed an interminable time, a flurry of impressions spun round his eyes.

At last, the time machine came to a halt, but he did not pause to see what was around him. He pressed the 'start' switch again.

Nothing happened. File inspected all the dials in turn, casting a long look at one which, as Appeltoft had told him, registered the machine's 'time-potential', that is, its capacity to travel through time.

The hand was at zero. He was stranded.

Thirty-three per cent of our test animals don't return. Appeltoft's remark slipped sardonically into his memory.

The cameras behind his shoulders were humming almost imperceptibly as they recorded the scene on micro-tape. Bleakly, File lifted his head and took stock of his surroundings.

The sight was beautiful but alien. The landscape consisted of sullen orange dust, over which roamed what looked like clouds – purple masses rolling and drifting over the surface of the desert. On the horizon of this barren scene, the outlines of grotesque architecture were visible – or were they just natural formations?

He glanced upwards. There were no clouds in the sky: evidently they were too dense to float in free air. A small sun hung low, red in a deep blue sky where stars were faintly visible.

His heart was beating rapidly: as he noticed this, he realized that he was breathing more deeply than usual, every third breath almost a gasp. Was he so far removed from his own time that even the atmosphere was different!

Skrrak! The sound came with a brittle, frail quality over the thin air. File turned his head, startled.

A group of bipeds was advancing, straggling on bony, delicate limbs through knee-deep strata of purple clouds which rolled in masses a few hundred yards away. They were humanoid, but skeletal, ugly, and clearly not human. The leader, who was over seven feet tall, was shouting and pointing at File and the machine.

Another waved his hands: *'So Skrrak – dek svala yaa!'*

The group, about ten in number, carried long slim spears and their torsos and legs were covered with scrubby hair. Their triangular heads had huge ridges of bone over and under the eyes so that they seemed to be wearing helmets. Thin hair swirled around their heads as they came closer, proceeding cautiously as if in slow motion.

As they approached, File saw that some of them carried curious rifle-like weapons, and the leader bore a box-shaped instrument with a lens-structure on one side, which he was pointing in his direction.

File felt the warmth of a pale green beam, and tried to dodge it. But the alien creature skilfully kept it trained on him.

After a second or two, a buzzing set up in his brain; fantastic colours engulfed his mind, separating out into waves of white and gold. Then geometric patterns flared behind his eyes. Then words – at first in his brain, and then in his ears.

'Strange one, what is your tribe?'

He was hearing the guttural language of the alien – and understanding it. The creature touched a switch on the top of the box, and the beam flicked off.

'I am from another time,' File said without emphasis.

The warriors shifted their weapons uneasily. The leader nodded, a stiff gesture, as if his bone structure did not permit easy movement. 'That would be an explanation.'

'Explanation?'

'I am conversant with all the tribes, and you do not correspond to any of them.' The warrior shifted his great head to give the horizon a quick scrutiny. 'We are the Yulk. Unless you intend to depart immediately, you had best come with us.'

'But my machine . . .'

'That also we will take. You will not wish it to be destroyed by the Raxa, who do not permit the existence of any creature or artifact save themselves.'

File debated for some moments. The chair and its three rods were easily portable, but was it wise to move them?

Idly, he moved the useless 'start' switch again. Damn! Since the machine no longer worked, what difference did it make if he moved it to the Moon? And yet to go off with these alien creatures when his only objective was to return to the Geneva Complex seemed the most obvious absurdity.

A sick feeling of failure came over him. He was beginning to realize that he was never going to get back to Geneva. The scientists had known that there was some fault in their time transmission methods; now, he knew, the chair with its three rods had lost all touch with the equipment in the laboratory. It was, in fact, no longer a time machine, and that meant he was doomed to stay here for the rest of his life.

Helplessly he gave his consent. A quartet of warriors picked up the chair and the party set off across the ochre desert, glancing warily about it as they travelled.

They skirted round the moving clouds wherever they could, but sometimes the banks of purple vapour swept over them, borne by the wide movements of the travelling breeze, and they stumbled through a vermilion fog. File noticed that the alien beings kept a tight hold on their weapons when this happened. What was it they feared? Even in this desolated and near-empty world, strife and dramas played themselves out.

An hour's journey brought them to a settlement of tents clustered on a low hillside. A carefully cultivated plot of some wretched vegetation grew over about half the hill, as though only just managing to maintain itself in the sterile desert. Tethered over the camp were five floating vessels, each about a hundred feet long, graceful machines with stubby, oblate sterns and tapered bows. A short open deck projected aft atop each vessel and the forward parts were laced with windows.

File's gaze lingered on these craft. They contrasted oddly

with the plainly nomadic living quarters below, cured animal hides with weak fires flickering among them.

A meal had just been prepared. File's time machine was taken to an empty tent and he was invited to eat with the chief. As he entered the largest tent of the settlement and saw the nobility of this small tribe gathered round a vegetable stew-pot with their weapons beside them, he knew what it was they reminded him of.

Lizards.

They began to eat from glass bowls. It seemed these people knew how to work the silicates of the desert as well as build flying ships – if they had not stolen them from some more advanced people.

In the course of the meal, File also discovered that the machine the warrior had trained on him in the desert was one hundred per cent efficient. He had been completely re-educated to talk and think in another language, even though he could, if he chose, detach himself slightly, hear the strangeness of the sounds which came from both his mouth and those of the Yulk.

The chief's name was Gzerhteak, an almost impossible sound to European ears. As they ate, he answered File's questions in unemotional tones.

From what he was told, he imagined that this was an Earth in old age, an Earth millions, perhaps billions of years ahead of his own time, and it was nearly all desert. There were about eight tribes living within a radius of a few hundred miles, and when they were not squabbling among themselves they were fighting a never-ending struggle for existence both with the ailing conditions of a dying world, and with the Raxa, creatures who were not organic life at all but consisted of mineral crystals conglomerated into geometrical forms, and, in some mysterious way, endowed both with sentience and the property of mobility.

'Fifty generations ago,' the Yulk chief told him, 'the Raxa had no existence in the world; then they began to grow. They thrive in the dead desert, which is all food for them, while we steadily die. There is nothing we can do, but fight.'

Furthermore, the atmosphere of the Earth was becoming unbreathable. Little fresh oxygen was being produced, since there was no vegetation except at the plantations. Beside this, noxious vapours were being manufactured by a chemical-geological action in the ground, and by slow volcanic processes which drifted through the sand from far below. Only in a few places, such as this region where the tribes lived, was the atmosphere still suitable for respiration, and that only because of the relative stillness of the atmosphere, which discouraged the separate gases from mixing.

It was a despairing picture of courage and hopelessness which gradually unfolded to File. Was this the final result of man's inability to control events, or was the collapse of the European Economic Community an insignificant happening which had been swallowed up by a vaster history? He tended to think that this was so; for he felt sure that the creatures who sat and ate with him were not even descended from human stock.

Lizards. The old order of the world of life had died away.

Men had gone. Only these fragments remained, lizards elevated to a manlike state, attempting to retain a foothold in a world which had changed its mind. Probably the other tribes the Yulk spoke of were also humanoids who had evolved from various lower animals.

'Tomorrow is the great battle,' the Yulk chief said. 'We throw all our resources against the Raxa, who advance steadily to destroy the last plantations on which we depend. After tomorrow, we shall know in our hearts how long we have to live.'

Max File clenched his hands impotently. His fate was sealed. Eventually he too would take his place alongside the Yulk warriors in the last stand against humanity's enemy.

Appeltoft spread his hands impassively and looked at Strasser. What could he do? He had done all he could.

'What happened?' said the Prime Minister.

'We tracked him ten years into the future. We got him on the start of his journey back, and then quite suddenly – gone. Nothing. I told you we lost thirty-three per cent of our experimental animals in the same way. I warned you of the risk.'

'I know – but have you tried everything? You know what it will mean if he doesn't return . . .'

'We have been trying, of course. We are searching now, trying to pick him up, but outside the Earth's time-track all is chaotic to our instruments – some defect in our understanding of time. We can probe out – but really, a needle in a haystack is nothing compared ...'

'Well, keep trying. Because if you don't get him back soon we shall be forced to allow the Untermeyer people to go ahead in Bavaria and we have no means of predicting the result.'

Appeltoft sighed wearily and returned to his laboratory.

When he had left the chamber, Standon said: 'Poor devil.'

'There's a time and a place for sentimentality, Standon,' Strasser said guiltily.

The Earth still rotated in the same period, and after a sleep of about eight hours File left his tent and stretched his limbs in the thin air, aroused by the sound of clinking metal. It was just after dawn, and the fighting males of the tribe were setting out to battle. The females and children, shivering, watched as their menfolk went off in procession into the desert. A few rode reptile-like horses, precious cossetted animals all of whom had been harnessed for the battle. Twenty feet above their heads the five aircraft floated patiently following the direction given by the chief below.

File hung around the camp, apprehensive and edgy. About an hour after sunset, the remnants of the forces returned.

It was defeat. A third of the men had survived. None of the aircraft returned, and File had learned the night before that although the tribe retained the knowlege and skill to build more, it was an undertaking that strained their resources to the utmost and the construction of another would almost certainly never begin.

Humanity's strength was depleted beyond revival point. The mineral intelligences called the Raxa would continue their implacable advance with little to stop them.

The Yulk chief was the last man in. Bruised, bleeding and scorched by near-misses from energy beams, he submitted to the medications of the women, and then called the nobles together as usual for their evening meal.

One by one, the wearied warriors took their leave and made their ways to their tents, until File was left alone with Gzerhteak.

He looked directly into the old man's eyes. 'There is no hope,' he said bluntly.

'I know. But there is no need for you to remain.'

'I have no choice.' He sighed. 'My machine has broken down. I must throw in my lot with you.'

'Perhaps we can repair your machine. But you will be

plunging into the unknown . . .'

File made a gesture with his hands. 'What could you possibly do to repair my machine!'

The chief rose and led the way to the tent where the machine lay. A brief command into the night produced a boy with a box of tools. The chief studied File's machine, lifting a panel to see behind the instruments. Finally, he made adjustments, adding a device which took him about twenty minutes to make with glowing bits of wire. The time-potential meter began to lift above zero.

File stared in surprise.

'Our science is very ancient and very wise,' the chief said, 'though these days we know it only by rote. Still, I, as father of the tribe, know enough so that when a man like yourself tells me that he has stranded himself in time, I know what the reason is.'

File was astounded by the turn of events. 'When I get home –' he began.

'*You will never get home.* Neither will your scientists ever analyse time. Our ancient science has a maxim: No man understands time. Your machine travels under its own power now. If you leave here, you simply escape this place and take your chance elsewhere.'

'I must make the attempt,' File said. 'I cannot remain here while there is a hope of getting back.'

But still he lingered.

The chief seemed to guess his thoughts. 'Do not fear that you desert us,' he said. 'Your position is clear – as is ours. There is no help for either of us.'

File nodded and stepped up to the chair of the machine. As he cleaned off the grime and dust with his shirt sleeves, it occurred to him to look at the date-register – he had not bothered to read the figures on his arrival. He did not expect it to make sense, for it had too few digits to account for the present antiquity of the Earth.

But when he read the dial he received a shock. 000008.324. 01.7954. Less than nine years after his departure from the Geneva Complex!

He seated himself on the time machine and pressed the switch.

Internal rotation clockwise . . . external rotation anti-clockwise ... then the forward rushing. He plunged into the continuum of Time.

Minutes passed, and no sign came that he would emerge automatically from his journey. Taking a chance, he pressed the switch to 'stop'.

With a residual turning of the translucent rods, the machine deposited itself into normal space-time orientation. About him, the landscape was more mind-shaking than anything he had ever dreamed.

Was it crystal? The final victory of the crystalline Raxa? For a moment the fantastic landscape, with its flashing, brilliant, mathematical overgrowth, deluded him into thinking it was so. But then he saw that it could not be – or if it was, the Raxa had evolved beyond their mineral heritage.

It was a world of geometrical form, but it was also a world of constant movement – or rather, since the movement was all so sudden as to be instantaneous, of constant transformation. Flashing extensions and withdrawals, all on the vertical and horizontal planes, dazzled his eyes. When he looked closer, he saw that in fact *three-dimensional form was nowhere present.* Everything consisted of two-dimensional shapes, which came together transitorily to give the *illusion* of form.

The colours, too ... they underwent transformations and graduations which bespoke the action of regular mathematical principles – like the prismatic separation into the ideal spectrum. But here the manifestations were infinitely more subtle and inventive, just as subtle, tenuous music, using fifty instruments, can be made out of the seven tones of the diatonic scale.

File looked at the date register. It told him he was now fifteen years away from Appeltoft, anxiously awaiting his return in the Geneva Complex.

He tried again.

A lush world of lustrous vegetation swayed and rustled in a hot breeze. A troop of armadillo-like animals, but the size of horses, paraded through the clearing where File's machine had come to rest. Without pausing, the leader swung its head to give him a docile, supercilious inspection, then turned to grunt something to the followers. They also gave him a cursory glance and then they had passed through a screen of wavy grass-trees. He heard their motions through the forest for some distance.

Again.

Barren rock. The sky hung with traceries of what were obviously dust-clouds. Here the ground was clean of even the slightest trace of dust, but a strong cold wind blew. Presumably it swept the dust into the atmosphere and prevented it from precipitating, scouring the rock to a sparkling, ragged surface. He could hardly believe that this scrubbed shining landscape was actually the surface of a planet. It was like an exhibit.

Again.

Now he was in space, protected by some field the time machine seemed to create around itself. Something huge as Jupiter hung where Earth should have been.

Again.

Space again. A scarlet sun pouring bloody light over him. On his left, a tiny, vivid star, like a burning magnesium flare, lanced at his eyes. An impossible three-planet tribune rotated majestically above him, with no more distance between them than from the Earth to the Moon.

He looked at the date register again. Twenty-odd years from departure.

Where was the sequence? Where was the progression he had come to find? How was Appeltoft to make sense out of this?

How was he going to find Appeltoft?

Desperately, he set the machine in motion again. His desperation seemed to have some effect: he picked up speed, rushing with insensate energy and now he was not just in limbo but could see something of the universe through which he was passing.

After a while he got the impression that he was still, that it was the machine that was static while time and space were not. The universe poured around him, a disordered tumult of forces and energies, lacking direction, lacking purpose...

On he sped, hour after hour, as if he were trying to flee from some fact he could not face. But at last, he could hide from it no longer. As he observed the chaos around him he *knew*.

Time *had* no sequence! It was *not* a continuous flowing. It had no positive direction: it went neither forwards, backwards, nor in a circle; neither did it stay still. *It was totally random.*

The universe was bereft of logic. It was nothing but chaos.

It had no purpose, no beginning, no end. It existed only as a random mass of gases, solids, liquids, fragmentary accidental patterns. Like a kaleidoscope, it occasionally formed itself into patterns, so that it *seemed* ordered, *seemed* to contain laws, *seemed* to have form and direction.

But, in fact, there was nothing but chaos, nothing but a constant state of flux – the only thing that was constant. There *were* no laws governing time! Appeltoft's ambition was impossible!

The world from which he had come, or any other world for that matter, could dissipate into its component elements at any instant, *or could have come into being at any previous instant, complete with everybody's memories!* Who would be the wiser? The whole of the European Economic Community might have existed only for the half-second which it had taken him to press the starting switch on the time machine. No wonder he couldn't find it!

Chaos, flux, eternal death. All problems were without solution. As File realized these facts he howled with horror of it. He could not bring himself to stop. In proportion to his despair and fear, his speed increased, faster and faster, until he was pouring madly through turmoil.

Faster, farther –

The formless universe around him began to vanish as he went to an immense distance and beyond the limits of speed. Matter was breaking up, disappearing. Still he rushed on in terror, until the time machine fell away beneath him, and the matter of his body disintegrated and vanished.

He was a bodiless intelligence, hurtling through the void. Then his emotions began to vanish. His thoughts. His identity. The sensation of movement dropped away. Max File was gone. Nothing to see, hear, feel, or know.

He hung there, nothing but consciousness. He did not think: he no longer had any apparatus to think with. He had no name. He had no memories. No qualities, attributes, or feelings. He was just *there*. Pure ego.

The same as nothing.

There was no time. A split second was the same as a billion ages.

So it would not have been possible for File, later, to assign any period to his interlude in unqualified void. He only became aware of anything when he began to emerge.

At first, there was only a vague feeling, like something misty. Then more qualities began to attach themselves to him. Motion began. Chaotic matter became distantly perceptible – disorganized particles, flowing energies and wavy lines.

A name impinged on his consciousness: Max File. Then the thought: That's me.

Matter gradually congregated round him and soon he had a body again and a complete set of memories. He could accept the existence of an unorganized universe now. He sighed: at the same moment the time machine formed underneath him.

All he could do now was to try to return to Geneva, however remote the possibility. How strange, to think that the whole of Europe, with all its seriously taken problems, was nothing more than a chance coming-together of random particles! But at least it was home – even if it only existed for a few seconds.

And if he could only rejoin those few seconds, he thought in agonized joyousness, he would be dissolved along with the rest of it and be released from this hideous extension of life he had escaped into.

And yet, he thought, how could he get back? Only by searching, only by searching...

He reckoned (though of course his calculations were liable to considerable error) that he spent several centuries searching through mindless turmoil. He grew no older; he felt no hunger or thirst: he did not breathe – how his heart kept beating without breath was a mystery to him, but it was on this, the centre of his sense of time, that he based his belief about the duration of the search. Occasionally he came upon other brief manifestations, other transient conglomerations of chaos. But now he was not interested in them, and he did not find Earth at the time of the E.E.C.

It was hopeless. He could search for ever.

In despair, he began to withdraw again, to become a bodiless entity and find oblivion, escape from his torments in the living death. It was while he was about to dispense with the last vestige of identity, that he discovered his unsuspected power.

He happened to direct his mind to a grouping of jostling particles some distance away. Under the impact of his will – it moved!

Interested, he halted his withdrawl, but did not try to emerge back into his proper self – he had the feeling that as Max File he was impotent. As an almost unqualified ego – perhaps...

He allowed an image to form in his mind – it happened to be that of a woman – directed it at the formless chaos. Instantly, against dark flux, lit by random flashes of light, a woman was formed out of chaotic matter. She moved, looked at him and gave a languorous smile.

There was no doubt about it. She was not just an image. She was alive, perfect, and aware.

Amazed, he automatically let go of the mental image and transmitted a cancellation. The woman vanished, replaced by random particles and energies as before. The cloud lingered for a moment, then dispersed.

It was a new-found delight. He could make anything! For ages he experimented, creating everything he could think of. Once, a whole world formed beneath him, complete with civilizations, a tiny sun, and rocket-ships probing out.

He cancelled it at once. It was enough to know that his every intention, even his vaguest and grandest thought, was translated into detail.

Now he had a means to return home – and now he could solve the government's problem for good and all.

For if he could not find Europe, could he not create it over again? Would that not be just as good? In fact, it was a point of philosophy whether it would not be in fact the same Europe. This was Nietzsche's belief, he remembered – his hope of personal immortality. Since, in the boundless universe, he was bound to recur – File's discoveries had reinforced this view, anyhow – he would not die. Two identical objects shared the same existence.

And in this second Europe, why should he not solve the government's dilemma for them? Was there any reason why he should not create a community which did not contain the seeds of destruction? An economic community with stability, which the prototype had lacked?

He began to grow excited. It would defeat Flux, stand against the chaos of the rest of the universe, containing a structure which would last. Otherwise, it would be the same in every detail...

He set to work, summoning up thoughts, memories, and images, impinging them in the surrounding chaos. Matter began to form. He set the time machine in motion, travelling on to the world he was creating...

Suddenly he was in mistiness again. Rotating ... rotation without change of position ... rushing forward...

The numbers clicked off his dial: 000008 – 7 – 6 – 5 – 4 . . .

Then everything steadied around him as the machine came to a stop. He was in Appeltoft's laboratory in Geneva. Technicians prowled the outskirts of the room, beyond the barriers of trestles. The time machine, its translucent rods pointing dramatically in three directions, rested on a rough wooden pedestal.

File moved, stiff, aching, and dusty, in the grimy seat. Appeltoft rushed forward, helping him down anxiously and delightedly.

'You're back on the dot, old man! As a test flight it was perfect – from our end.' He flicked his finger over his shoulder, 'Bring brandy for the man! You look done in, Max. Come and clean up; then you can tell us how it went . . .'

File nodded, smiling wordlessly. It was almost perfect . . . but he had not realized just how efficiently he had been taught a new language.

Appeltoft had spoken to him in the voice-torturing tongue of the Yulk.

Schmeling came back into the half-light of his sitting room and placed his graceful, bulky body into the armchair opposite mine.

'Sorry to have left you so abruptly,' he said, in reference to the phone call which had taken him from the room.

'You seem excited,' I said, noting the look of jubilation in his eyes.

'I am,' he said. 'Indeed, I am.'

I had to leave it at that, for he didn't seem prepared to talk about it.

He seemed to dismiss whatever he was thinking about and gave me a quick smile. 'Well, how are things in sociological circles?'

'Going in circles for me at present,' I said good-humouredly. 'I've a particularly interesting case right now. By all the evidence – environment, family background, I.Q., and so on – he should fit neatly into a certain broad category. But he doesn't. He shows, in his thinking and behaviour, all the classic symptoms of an under-privileged slum child from a split home – whereas, in fact, his background is almost the opposite.'

Schmeling appeared only mildly interested in my work, yet he caught hold of something I said and it set him off on another track.

'So? You really think that all these superficial influences have a deep effect on an individual?'

'Normally, yes. And I don't consider them superficial. They can have a deep and lasting significance for a person.'

He smiled patronizingly. 'I consider so-called inherited traits also superficial – not to say non-existent.'

'It astounds me!' I said lightly. Schmeling seemed about to indulge in one of his conversational exercises where he would take a dogmatic stand on a point about which he had little serious interest. Such an exercise was often entertaining and I prepared to join in his mood by taking an equally dogmatic stand against him.

Schmeling waved his hand. 'We talk of heredity as a fact

and we talk of mutual experience as a fact. Yet how much experience *is* shared?'

'All of it,' I said immediately.

Schmeling's large, aquiline head nodded thoughtfully, and then he glanced at me with undue seriousness. 'People find it easy to ascribe a pattern to the human psyche, for there are many such superficial similarities between men. I believe, however, that we'd rather accept a pattern that explains things comfortably, than attempt to grasp the idea of the infinite variety and complexity of human experience. A variety limited only to the number of individuals existing on the world. And I contend that each man is, mentally and physically, a total individual – unique.'

'There is no such thing as an individual,' I pointed out. 'There are minor superficial differences in behaviour, that is all.'

'I say there are minor superficial similarities which we have come to accept as constituting the *total* human psyche. There are depths, my friend, which haven't begun to be explored. And also,' he said, with a note of slight triumph in his voice, 'how would you explain the increase, during this century, in advanced schizophrenia? No two schizophrenics are alike.'

'That's debatable,' I said.

Schmeling grimaced. 'And I have heard you call yourself an individualist!'

'So I am – within certain limitations,' I said, a trifle over-warmly.

'You *are* an individual,' he replied, leaning back in his chair and sticking his feet before the fire. I could see he was beginning to enjoy the argument, which meant he was fairly certain of winning it.

'You are, indeed,' he emphasized. 'The very impossibility of our ever fully communicating with one another proves that conclusively. How much time is an elephant?'

'Eh?'

'Can you answer?'

'The question is nonsense!'

'To you, perhaps, but not to people who see time in terms of mass – and many do. Recent experiments have shown that the question receives as many answers as there are individuals asked it. There are many other pointers to prove my case – the people who see Sunday as a particular colour whereas others see it as a line of particular length – everything seen with the *mind*'s eye, heard with the *mind*'s ear, inhaled with the *mind*'s nose, touched with the *mind*'s touch, tasted with the *mind*'s palate means something entirely different to everyone! That, I contend, is where reality lies – in the *mind*'s senses, where we experience what we want to experience – not what we are told to!'

'This conversation still leads nowhere,' I said. 'Abstract questions regarding man's nature can only produce abstract answers.'

'True,' he eyed me triumphantly, as if he had deliberately provoked me into an admission, 'but when a concrete solution appears, it has the effect of making the problem concrete also. Do you agree?'

'Yes.'

'Well, I received concrete proof, not long ago, of the *fact* that each man does exist as an individual – totally, irreversibly – that, although environment and "heredity" act upon him from birth, they act to make him appear a non-individual. You see the difference? He begins as a *whole* individual but superficial influences force him not to be, do you see?'

'You would say that society imposes a pattern on the individual which we regard as inherent but you see as superficial. I think I follow you. Your extreme example would be the suburbanite who conforms rigorously, I suppose?'

'More tragic examples could be made – the Zeitgeist dominating Germany in the thirties, for instance.' He paused, seeming to consider his native country which he had left so many years before. 'A German word,' he mused, 'to describe the German Disease – the need to inflict patterns and generalizations on every aspect of human existence. The insidious Freud must have found German a ready-made language for his doctrines. A language with so many words which are, in reality, unspecific, leads to the kind of unspecific thinking I find so abhorrent.'

He shrugged and nodded. 'But the suburban man is a fair example.'

He got up. His large, vital body tensed in the manner of an actor about to deliver an oratory, but instead of speaking immediately, he left me in suspense while he helped himself to some of his horrible herbal tobacco from a box on the sideboard. When the deed was done, the metal-stemmed pipe alight and the sweet smoke, so much less pleasant than ordinary tobacco, invading my nostrils, he resumed his seat by the fire.

'And perhaps the schizophrenic psychopath – the rebel without a cause – is the extreme example of the individual who experiences the obvious wrongness of this conformism and reacts against it violently.'

'A million suburbanites can't be wrong,' I said ironically, and he smiled around the clenched pipe.

'A single psychopath can't be wrong, either. A single psychopath, according to his own little universe, is absolutely right, absolutely justified in taking any course of action he chooses – simply because *he* chooses it!'

'But unfortunately, this attitude works to produce anarchy,' I said. 'If he doesn't conform to a certain degree, his actions interfere with other people's actions producing either chaos if he is successful, or else further curtailment of his liberty. I'm right.'

'To a degree you're right,' he nodded. 'But if everyone accepted the individual's right to be an individual and the tyranny of conformism were lifted, perhaps we could give a greater dignity to existence – and still work together in the manner of individuals aiding individuals...'

'We're coming close to talking politics,' I warned him with a smile, adding: 'Or religion – the two unprovables.'

'Both attract psychopaths, at any rate. Witness the fact that both religious and political movements are notoriously inclined to break into almost as many splinter-groups as there are individuals comprising them.'

'All facts,' I agreed. 'But you said you'd received concrete proof that all men are unequal!'

'I did not – as far as "equality" enters into this argument, I would say I had proved that all men *are* equal, in that all men are different and existing,' he paused dramatically, and I envied him, his poise, his resonant voice, 'existing in *physically* different universes!'

'Oh, come now...'

'Time and space are relative. And the time and space of the individual are relative to that of other individuals. But they are not the *same*. I have proof that every man exists in his own space-time continuum as well as in the larger one we all share. Why is it that for one man an hour passes slowly and for another it passes rapidly?'

'His state of mind at the time he's experiencing the hour's

passage, surely?'

'His state of mind – exactly. He imposes his own time sense on the time he is *told* is the right one.'

'What of this assertion of proof?' I said, feeling the conversation to be losing its dynamic.

'Very well,' he said, glancing at his watch. He shifted in his chair and began in the manner of a story-teller, choosing all his phrases with care. I also settled myself, expecting to be entertained, for Schmeling is a good talker who only requires an attentive audience to bring forth his skill.

A few months ago (he said in his deep, faintly-accented voice) I was enjoying a leisurely day at my Harley Street surgery, dispensing sympathy and disguised aspirin to the elderly women who finance my private research, when my hag of a receptionist entered in haste, a rare feat for one of her age. My clients resent young receptionists.

'Mrs Thornton is in the waiting room,' she croaked.

'But she has no appointment,' I said in irritation. These women are either hypochondriacs or else incurable. I choose them with care since both involve me in little real work.

Mrs Thornton was a little of both – an incurable hypochondriac, an otherwise charming woman in late middle-age, very rich and still vivacious whenever she took time off from her self-induced spells of migraine. Yes, she was, indeed, very rich, and also I quite liked her. Therefore, after a moment's deliberation, I told my receptionist to keep her waiting for a while and then show her in.

In a practice like mine it does not do to answer a patient's surprise visit immediately. If they conclude you are at the beck and call of every Tom, Dick, or Harry, they feel unimpressed by your skill as a doctor.

So, finally, Mrs Thornton was shown in, all delicious fur and a trifle too much expensive perfume. Her face was skilfully made-up and her tinted grey hair beautifully arranged. But I noted that she was distraught, glimpsed the smallest smear of mascara in the corner of her right eye.

She, the poised Mrs Thornton, appeared to have been crying in public.

I rose and indicated a chair for her to sit in. She sat on its edge.

'You seem to be in pain, Mrs Thornton,' I said solicitously, feeling that she had wished a particularly bad migraine upon herself.

'Not physical, Doctor Schmeling,' said she, 'but doubtless the emotional pain I am suffering will result in another migraine.'

Again I felt irritated.

My patients have a tendency to bring their emotional problems to me and expect me to treat them. Mind you, a receptive ear is usually sufficient, and a soft and ambiguous word of consolation. So, I prepared myself to hear her out, making a mental note to append this consultation on to another bill in the near future.

'Now calm yourself,' I said in the gruff and kindly voice which at once commands the impression of professional integrity and human warmth.

'Tell me the trouble, before you ask me to clear it up.'

She smiled a small smile of thanks, responding beautifully to the emotional cues I was feeding her.

'It is my nephew, doctor, who is in trouble, not I.'

'He is ill?'

I have a dislike of treating male patients since there is a greater chance of them penetrating my facade, so necessary if I am to be allowed to continue my private work. Yet I prepared myself for the worst, since Mrs Thornton's contribution was that much larger than my other patients.

'Not physically,' Mrs Thornton gave me the melting look of one who confides in a friend and expects help.

'Mentally,' I hinted, with just the right tactful emphasis.

She nodded mutely.

'But, my dear Mrs Thornton, you must understand that I am not a psychologist – I am a simple physician . . .' I was, of course, lying since although I am qualified as a physician, my work in fact centres upon understanding the psychological quirks of my clientele.

'I know, I know,' she said eagerly, 'but you are so *understanding*, doctor, in my own case. You realize that migraine is caused by *mental* and *nervous* and *emotional* stresses, so I thought . . .'

I controlled the tendency to smile. All migraine sufferers are inclined to ascribe non-physical causes to their condition, when, as often as not, a simple physical act of bending down or eating the wrong food is the cause of that admittedly exacting complaint.

Instead, I nodded sternly and kindly. 'True, true, true,' muttered I in the mystical manner of so many psychiatrists –

hinting at things which only the fully enlightened disciple of Freud might learn. There is no doubt about it. They are the new priesthood.

'Then – for my sake, doctor – come and see him. Try to help him. And I beg you to use discretion in this matter – a public scandal would result if . . .'

'Of course,' I said conspiratorially, 'and if I cannot help him I can recommend an extremely discreet friend – a specialist in mental disorders – a wonderful man, I assure you, of undoubted brilliance and integrity.'

But it was I whom she wanted. I prepared myself to act out a particularly long part. Have you noticed how people act, quite unconsciously, in set ranges of expression and emotion which fit particular categories – Sympathetic, Righteous Indignation, Bewildered Grief and so on, when in fact beneath the surface, though they do not for a moment admit it to themselves, they feel nothing of what they express on the surface? Gestures, gestures – bolstering up the inane meaninglessness of modern life. And thanks to modern communications, we are assured, more and more, of the Right Way To Feel In A Given Situation. Comforting – certainly, comforting. Good God, we are like water-beetles skating the slimy surface which covers the clear, pure water below. And, worse, we contribute to the extent and thickness of the slime, piling it higher and higher until, with any luck, we shall sink down with its weight to the bottom. What do you think will happen then? Madness? But I digress.

Mrs Thornton's town house lay in a quiet Belgravian Square. I drove her there myself, leaving a note to my receptionist to re-arrange the rest of the day's appointments.

Two marble columns fronted the main entrance and we went through the heavy oak door into a chill and imposing hallway, also of the same barren marble. We gave our street clothes to an attractive little maid and Mrs Thornton asked her where Mr Davenport was.

'In the study, ma'am,' the maid replied with a worried glance at me.

'Would you tell him that I have brought Doctor Schmeling and should like to see him in the drawing room?'

We entered the large, light drawing room which was fashionably furnished in a slightly Victorian manner. A heavy secretaire had been converted into a cocktail cabinet and from this Mrs Thornton offered me a drink. I accepted a dry sherry and stood sipping it while we awaited Nicholas Davenport. Mrs. Thornton moved nervously about the room for a moment before sitting down on the arm of a chair.

Nicholas entered, pale, disconsolate, defiant. A black-haired youth of a distinctly wild appearance, shaking me too firmly by the hand as we were introduced and going immediately to the cabinet and pouring himself a drink. I expected him to disclaim need of a doctor, but instead he turned, still with a defiant look in his eye, and said 'I hope to God you can do something about this, doctor.' The defiance, it seemed, was permanent and directed at the world in general rather than any single individual.

'Perhaps I can,' I said, eyeing him a little warily, wondering what he would make of me. 'Would you care to tell me your trouble?'

'Troubles,' he said, taking a romantic stance by the curtains.

This, I decided with enjoyment, was to be a play of high drama. But, at that moment, I underestimated Davenport. I was to learn that he was a good actor, in the sense you know me to mean, but, for some reason, had hopelessly garbled his lines, lost his cues – or at least imposed his own lines and cues upon a play which resented them and was discomforted by them. My first hint of this came very soon after Mrs Thornton had tactfully left the room and he and I stood facing one another across its length, drinks in hand in the manner of duellists about to stand and fire.

'Doctor Schmeling, you are not, I understand, a psychologist?'

'No, I am a physician. I have a certain private bent towards psychology, though. However, if you wish to consult a qualified man...'

'No, no – I'm sorry, but I'm afraid a man not fully conversant with – mental disorders – might dismiss what I tell him as nonsense.'

Curious, I shook my head. 'That won't happen,' I told him, 'but I may be forced to recommend a specialist if I do not feel competent to deal with your case.'

'Fair enough,' he said. 'I am having illusions.'

I restrained an urge to discourse philosophically on the meaning of the word and instead raised my eyebrows. 'What kind of illusions, Mr Davenport?'

'Many kinds. Illusions of complete physical detachment, where my mind looks down on my body and observes it with clinical objectivity. Illusions of size where I am sometimes so small as to be a pin-prick in the vastness of infinite space and at the same time am so huge as to dwarf the universe. Illusions of hearing voices speaking phrases I might not hear for days later, or should have heard days before; illusions where a place is familiar though I have never before visited it – *déja vu*, I believe it is called – illusions where a place I have known for years, this house for instance, becomes suddenly unfamiliar as if I am seeing it for the first time. Those are a few – just a very few, doctor.'

I frowned thoughtfully. The illusions he had mentioned were, in fact, all of a kind. They were what we call 'hypnagogic images' – the illusions experienced while falling asleep – the illusions between being awake and being asleep, between sleeping and dreaming. I have read that these illusions closely resemble those induced by mescaline and the like.

'We are all subject to illusions of this kind,' I said reluctantly, disappointed that his complaint was so undramatic after all. 'I myself sometimes get them.'

'Ah, yes,' he nodded rapidly, '*sometimes*. Sometimes, doctor. But do you get them all the time? Are you forced, as I am forced now, to exercise a rigid and deliberate control upon yourself, to force yourself to behave normally, to converse reasonably and logically, to walk a few yards to a shop to buy a newspaper, to consciously exert tremendous concentration if you are to see that newspaper in your hands and read it?'

'No, of course not.' I felt excited then.

'Of course not.' His pale face tautened and he drew his lips tight and wetted them and continued. 'Some time ago, under circumstances mildly resembling those I have described, I came across the source of a much used quotation. A poem by John Donne – that glib fool and mystic – "No man is an island" – you remember it, of course, with its preaching pantheistic nonsense. Well, I am an island, doctor – cut off from my fellow men most of the time by seas more uncrossable than the vastness of intergalactic space – I am an island existing in my *own* space, my *own* time – in fact, in my own universe which has little contact with the universe around it!'

You must understand that at this time, though interested, I was not convinced, as now, of what is literally physical individuality. I was at a loss for something to say for a moment. I could only mouth a trade-phrase.

'And when did you begin to experience all this?' I asked him.

'Some years ago,' he said impatiently. 'At first, as you pointed out, only between wakefulness and sleeping, then between sleeping and waking, then they continued through the morning, then all day and all night. I am not insane, doctor. I know I am not. But I shall soon go mad with the strain of keeping myself anchored to reality.'

'Do something for me, now,' I told him. 'Let loose your grip so that I can, as it were, observe the symptoms as I would an ordinary medical case.'

'Let loose ... doctor, I am even unsure that I could regain it if I did.' He seemed to think for a moment and then looked up at me, the defiance fading from his eyes to be replaced by the startling look of pleading which I have seen in the dying man afraid of death. 'If it means you will be able to cure me, I'll do it.'

'I cannot guarantee that until I have seen what it is,' I said, almost as intense as he.

'Then, by God, see!'

His face muscles seemed to relax to such an extent that his whole face appeared to lengthen. He staggered and I helped him into a deep armchair.

'I have told you, aunt, I have no wish to see a psychiatrist,' he said. His aunt, of course, was not in the room. Was he reliving the discussion which had led to Mrs Thornton consulting me?

Then I stepped back as he rose from the chair and began a peculiar and disturbing pantomime. I have seen similar scenes in cases of extreme shock where the patient re-enacts the phase leading up to traumatic experience again and again. Yet there was something odd even about this.

His lips were forming sentences, but I could not hear what he said. Then he went through the motions of taking off all his clothes, although his real clothes remained on his body. Then he seated himself.

He seated himself firmly upon thin air!

Astonished, not to say frightened, I rushed towards him and gripped him, sank to one knee and felt the air beneath him, saw that his feet were slightly lifted from the ground.

Then his arms moved and his head lolled upon his chest as if he had become unconscious.

I could not stand there and watch any longer, but seized

him and shook him begging him to wake up.

His eyes opened and he stared about him, but seemed not to see me.

'Doctor,' he said, 'I believe you have done it.' But he stared beyond me and to my left, addressing some unseen image of myself, perhaps.

Before I entirely lost my own grip, I again grasped his shoulders and spoke urgently into his ear.

'Davenport – Davenport – it is Doctor Schmeling – you are in the drawing room of your aunt's house. Can you hear me? Can you understand?'

Slowly his pale face turned and his body trembled in my hands. Once again the muscles stiffened as he stared, with difficulty, at me.

'I understand you. I remember. But what did I do? There seems to be no memory of...'

'Listen,' I said urgently. 'I want you to come with me and visit a close friend of mine – a physicist named King – this is not a case for psychologists or physicians, I am sure. We will go to see him now – will you come?'

'Will he help me?'

'If anyone can, King will help you,' I promised wildly.

'Very well.'

I told Mrs Thornton some vague story of needing to examine her nephew at my surgery and bundled him into my car, driving across London and out beyond Greenwich to the Special Research Institute of which King is the director.

Soon we were in King's office and had told him everything I knew. Then he listened to Davenport's story.

'You were right to come here,' he said. 'And I'm grateful, Schmeling, for you know we are currently doing research into the different degrees of physical awareness. We have several psychologists working with us, of course, and together we may be able to help Mr Davenport as well as,' he smiled at me, 'gaining some valuable information from any experiments we may have to instigate in order to find a cure.'

'So I'm to be a guinea-pig, is that it?' Davenport said bitterly.

'Yes,' King replied, 'but you must remember that the more we learn about your – um – affliction, the easier will be the task of helping you to readjust to reality.'

Soon afterwards it was arranged with Mrs Thornton that Nicholas Davenport should remain at the Research Institute until such a time as he was cured. We promised utmost secrecy and indeed were pleased to have it, since Davenport's condition was so astounding that any hint of it reaching the hungry ears of the sensational press would bring us untold irritation from journalists and cranks.

Time passed until, between them, King and his team had constructed a machine – a beautiful specimen – capable of recording Davenport's experiences while he underwent his illusions and of pulling him back, to some degree at least, to reality.

The data mounted, was sorted and investigated, until slowly we came close to arriving at certain conclusions regarding the nature of Davenport's problem.

Not only did Davenport dwell in a private universe, scarcely related to our commonly-shared time and space, but, if left entirely within it we observed it taking a definite course and shape so that, to himself, his existence had logical progression through both time and space. His past, present, and future experiences were arranged in a perfectly orderly manner save for one thing – his past experiences sometimes existed in our future and his present or future experiences often existed in our past.

Now, up to this point, we had investigated only Nicholas Davenport and it was possible that he was a freak, that no others like him existed. But we had to put this to the test – and I volunteered to be the control. By this time, their experiments with the first machine had enabled them to create another which might, if it worked according to the principle they had devised, have the effect of flinging me into what we were beginning to call 'the permanent hypnagogic state.'

The machine was a masterpiece, producing in the human metabolism the controllable effects of certain drugs like mescalin, lysergic acid or andrenolutin, by exercising a direct electronic control on both mind and blood-stream.

Whatever happened, I was assured of some interesting personal experiences.

I seated myself in a chair while the machine was focused upon my body. A recording device, of the kind I have mentioned, was also present.

The tests began.

The illusions were quite clear – in fact considerably sharper than most every-day experiences – they involved voice, pictures, actions, smells, and my sense of touch as well as certain mildly ecstatic emotional states which could turn swiftly to mildly depressed states. But then, this jumble began to sort itself out, the impressions and illusions began to form a definite pattern until I felt I was living an ordered life, scarcely different from the one I normally followed, save that I seemed to *know* better what it was all about, seemed, if you like, more at home in it.

Now, I learned later, I was released from my chair and allowed to wander around and was then confronted by Davenport in a similar state.

I saw him quite clearly, yet sensed absolutely no involvement with him, had no desire to approach him or interfere verbally or physically with his personal existence. However, after a time, he approached me and said politely:

'So you are free, too, Doctor Schmeling. Doubtless we were deliberately brought together in some way, but if we are allowed to continue in this state I look forward to communicating with you in some period when the time and space of the universe are favourable to another meeting – perhaps we have met already, in your past and my future?'

'Not yet,' I replied.

You see the new state of our existence? Without being directly involved, we were living in what were virtually wholly separate private universes. The nature of time had changed – or at least we had changed in relation to its nature – and it was quite possible for one individual to remember a meeting which had not yet taken place for another individual! We were free! Absolutely free and living what, I am convinced, is man's real and natural existence. Whatever freak occurrence on Earth ever set us off on the wrong road, I do not know. But now the truth was entirely clear. The fumblings of mystics, philosophers, and scientists towards this revelation had been forestalled by the world at large for centuries.

We conducted similar tests on large groups. King was as excited as I. We made no attempt to 'cure' Davenport and, once he understood what had happened to him, what must have happened to the thousands of poor 'schizophrenics' and 'victims of insanity' locked up all over the world, he accepted his condition as being normal – and our conditions as being abnormal.

Watching the experiments on the large groups, we saw Paradise – we saw Heaven, my friend – bands of angels living a peaceful and ordered personal existence – freed from the chains of so-called conformity, from the position of actors playing parts in a bad play, to real men performing real actions with meaning and absolute relevance to their personal existence. More – this state precludes any interference with the lives of their fellows.

It is what politicians have been shouting about for years and never achieving.

Thanks to young Nicholas Davenport, we have achieved the release of mankind from the slavery of togetherness. The tribe will go, the nation will go – there will be only independent men and women.

Schmeling leaned towards me, his heavy, aquiline head jutting forward, his large, square-tipped fingers spread upon the woven material of the armchair.

'Freedom,' he repeated. 'True Freedom!'

But I did not share his exultation. I was, in fact, horrified by the idea. It was impossible, to begin with. But the concept alone – the irresponsible concept – was enough to make me angry. I controlled myself as best I could.

'A good yarn, Schmeling,' I tried to smile. 'You were at your best. But really, man, the very idea of such an existence is appalling to an intelligent man. Society as we understand it would crumble – without organization we cannot have civilization – we could not have buildings, or railways or even newspapers.'

'But we could have books – books that one man produces lovingly upon his own press!'

'How many books? And how would they be distributed? How would he get his ink, his type, his spare parts for his press? Who would read them, anyway?'

'What do you mean?'

'Have animals any desire to read books, Schmeling?'

'That is irrelevant!'

'Oh, no – because the state you are holding up as desirable is an animal existence, don't you see?'

'Your vision is limited,' he said, seeming deliberately to relax in his chair. 'The kind of communication I speak of needs no books, anyway. It is a state of ecstacy, man – heaven on earth. It is what we have been promised for years!'

'Very well, you need no books. But man does not live by books alone – he lives by bread, too!'

'The individual finds the vitamins he needs by – well, by a

kind of instinct I can't explain.'

I laughed openly at this naive statement from a learned physician.

'I'm sorry, Schmeling, but our conversation is fast becoming ridiculous. I became too involved in your tale. Let's forget about all this talk of "perfect states" and "transcendental experience" before we wind up like two old Indian priests quarrelling in a monastery.'

But he did not respond to my desire to drop the subject before the argument became bitter and threatened our friendship.

'No,' he insisted. 'Look at it this way – you're a humane and liberal man, are you not? You give the individual a right to holding his own ideas so long as they do not harmfully interfere with another individual.'

I nodded without really listening, for I was bored with the argument.

'Ideas are large or small according to the individual,' he continued. 'You'd agree that if we criticize his ideas according to our own scale, we are wronging that man?'

'Yes.'

'Just as it is possible that an infinite number of things occupy the same space as our planet, having space and time as we have but otherwise existing in a different set of dimensions, so I know that every human being has "dimensions" individual to him. There are many instances where common dimensions are shared, but because this is true we have no business to conclude that therefore *all* dimensions are shared! Therefore you must concede that Man's right to be an individual is as much a physical necessity as it is a philosophical necessity. That to accept the shared dimensions as the only important or "real" ones and to reject those individual *to* the individual as "unnatural" or "wrong" is to deny a *physical truth*!'

'Come now, Schmeling. You have become too caught up in your speculation and yarn-spinning to continue with all this. Calm down, fill your pipe, and I'll be off in a moment or two. I never, I must admit, expected to hear a man of your intellect and common-sense talking so wildly. What you have postulated is total anarchy – an abhorrent state for any thinking creature. Thank God it is not so.'

I glanced with curiosity at Schmeling who had completely relaxed and was filling his pipe as I'd suggested. He chuckled to himself, as if over a private joke.

'You see I am right.' I smiled, rising.

'You'll see that I am right.' he chuckled.

'What do you mean?'

'Why, my dear chap, we have built several such machines of the kind I described. Large ones. They are set up at strategic points the world over. Within a few hours, we shall be flooding the planet with their effect – and real life will begin for man – the New Era – the era of salvation!'

I could take no more.

Shocked and disturbed at seeing so fine a mind behaving so childishly, I returned home. But I could not rid myself of a half-conviction that he had been speaking the truth all along.

I am home now and sitting in my study these write to notes analyse was in it whatever my fostered that conviction order...

WAITING FOR THE END OF TIME . . .

Chill winds blew over Tanet-tur-Taac and the salt stink of the sea was in Suron's nostrils through all the night and all the day because the waters were rising as the moon sank down.

Chill winds shredded the clouds above Tanet and sometimes they brought snow and sometimes they brought hot rain and sometimes they merely made waves on the sea.

His long hair floating in the wind, Suron-riel-J'ryec stared up at the moon and beyond it to Kadel Star which had once been so far away from Tanet, last world on the Rim. There were many large stars in the sky now and soon they and their planets would be one huge body. Tanet, too, would soon be part of that body.

From where he stood on the city's tallest tower Suron could see the distant mountains and now he altered his vision to bring some particular area into sharper perspective. He was sure he had seen something moving there again. But the wind was stirring the snow on the slopes. Perhaps that had been all he had seen.

Suron looked behind him at the slender towers of the city which was called Rion-va-mëy – Inevitable Hope – a city which was also a machine. Suron had built Rion-va-mëy and he had named the city-machine which had been designed to make Tanet a world completely independent of its sun, to shift it away from the pull of the Mass before it became too strong, to cross intergalactic space and find a galaxy still in equilibrium. That was why they had chosen this stark Rim world for their experiment, because it was the last habitable world on the edge of the galaxy.

And the galaxy was doomed to undergo a monstrous change in which nothing would remain as it had been.

The galaxy was condensing.

They had known it would since their scientists had come to understand the nature of the huge, dark bodies which lay at the centre of the galaxy. Megaquasars with a mass so great that even photons could not escape them, they had begun to increase their mass with every body which entered their gravitational field.

And now the entire galaxy lay within that field and each sun and its satellites were inexorably being drawn in as the mega-quasars consolidated into a single mass so vast that no real name could be invented for it. To most who referred to it at all it was just the Mass.

Suron watched the sky again as the day grew swiftly darker. His scheme had failed as it became clear that it was too late. Rion-va-mëy was the most sophisticated machine mankind had ever invented. Capable of providing a complete artificial environment, of shifting a planet as easily as a spacecraft, it could never be used for its original purpose. All it could do now was help Tanet to avert the inevitable collision for a few extra days.

It hardly functioned as a city now, for most of its citizens had departed when they realized Suron's scheme had failed. They had hoped to reach their home worlds before they were swallowed by their suns which would, in turn, be swallowed by larger suns before the Mass swallowed the whole.

Suron had remained, for Tanet was his world now. He loved it. And the one who loved Suron stayed with him.

The process had been gradual at first. A few thousand years ago it had scarcely been noticeable. A thousand years ago it had become plain what was happening. A hundred years ago half the suns and planets in the galaxy had been absorbed by the Mass and now the suns and planets of the Rim were moving towards each other.

A few more days, thought Suron, and we shall be on that last inward journey. And in less than a year, if the scientists' theories were correct, the Mass would collapse under the weight of its own gravitation and the entropic process would begin again. New stars, new planets, a new cycle.

Would the cycle repeat itself? Suron wondered. Was the galaxy programmed to form and re-form for eternity? Would mankind be reborn and recreate its history for perhaps the millionth time?

From the top of the tallest tower, his pale body exposed to the elements he savoured, Suron watched the waters. They had already reached some of the more distant structures. Again he looked at the Moon which now dominated the sky. It was a little closer than it had been yesterday, just as Tanet was a little closer to her sun, just as the stars gathered into a slightly tighter grouping.

Not long, he thought.

The short night passed. The sky's colour changed from deep blue to violet to a pale green and the clouds raced away over the horizon and were gone. The sun loomed over the horizon and Suron instantly felt its heat.

There was a whisper of sound behind Suron.

'So it was all for nothing.'

Mis'rn-bur-Sen placed a gentle hand on Suron's arm. 'The sun is closer, Suron.'

Suron turned and smiled at his husband.

'I dreamed, last night, of mankind. What was all for nothing?'

Mis'rn walked to the balustrade. Like Suron's, his skin was transparent and revealed the veins and organs of his hermaphroditic body. His pale hair waved in the warm wind.

'All the strife and the misery and the death. All the efforts of those who aspired to help mankind attain the tranquillity and security which we gained so recently. All wasted, Suron. Mankind has been cheated. At the moment of its triumph over its condition – over mortality, over its environment – nature still plays her jokes, still manages to find a way to destroy us.'

Suron smiled. 'A somewhat anthropomorphic view of the universe. Is it not enough to know that mankind did, eventually, triumph – did attain what the ancients called "a state of grace"? Is not the affection which you and I have something of a reward for all those millennia of struggle?'

Mis'rn bowed his head. 'Perhaps.'

The tower trembled. The sky darkened as new clouds came sweeping over the horizon. The roar of the sea drowned the sound of the wind. Suron put the tip of one long finger on the balustrade and drew a sign.

The bite of the wind and the bellowing of the sea were shut out as a field of energy formed an invisible dome over the tower. In the new silence Suron and Mis'rn stared into each other's large eyes.

'But our children are dead,' said Mis'rn at length.

Each had borne the other's child simultaneously some fifty years earlier. Both children had remained on the planet where they had been born and both now had been consumed.

Suron had accepted this fact without bitterness but Mis'rn, whose temperament was complementary to Suron's, still grieved.

And that was why Suron comforted his husband now.

Wordlessly he expressed his sympathy and wordlessly Mis'rn communicated his gratitude. The tower shook again.

'What was your dream of mankind?' Mis'rn asked.

'I do not remember the images, merely the mood. I stood here and I dreamed and then I awakened and, Mis'rn, I was happy.'

'You have shared that with me. I wish that I could have such a dream. But my dreams, when they come, are all of conflict and disaster.'

Suron pointed to the mountains. 'After my dream I thought I saw something moving on the slopes yonder. Perhaps it was part of the dream.'

'I think so. We are the last two to remain on Tanet. And there are no beasts here. Our ancestors saw to that.'

'And yet I had an impulse to go to the mountains – to see.'

'It is too dangerous, Suron. All the city's energy is being used to resist the pull of our sun and to keep our moon from falling into us. If you left its environs it could not protect you.'

'I know.'

Suron took Mis'rn's hand and whispered a sound.

They were transported into the heart of the tower, to a room of soft, ever-changing light which beamed nourishment into their systems. Then they made sweet, tender love – scarcely touching each other as they moved about the room in a graceful ballet of emotion.

And the tower trembled once more and the light flickered for an instant before resuming its transformations.

Mis'rn paused in his dance and Suron saw that there were the traces of a forgotten emotion beginning to emerge on his face. The emotion was fear.

'We must accept this, Mis'rn,' he said. 'We named this city Inevitable Hope because it was inevitable that we should hope. But now that hope is lost, we must accept it.'

'I cannot,' Mis'rn murmured. 'Suron, I cannot.'

Suron crossed the room and embraced him. 'Put yourself into sleep,' he suggested. 'Cut off the objective world entirely. It might heal you.'

'I have not done that since childhood.'

'But do it now, Mis'rn. Sleep helped our ancestors in this way when they could not tolerate the implications of reality. That was why they slept.'

'I will try.'

Suron traced a particular sign on the wall of light and the air in the centre of the room shivered and whispered and a couch appeared.

Mis'rn went to the couch and lay down, staring up at Suron.

'Close your eyes,' Suron said, and Mis'rn closed them. 'I will come and wake you,' Suron promised.

And Suron returned to the top of the tower, blinking in the intense light. He caused the dome to darken so that he could peer out at the landscape.

The snow had melted on the mountains. The sea moved moodily around the lower towers. The monstrous sun marched across the sky.

Suron focused his eyes so that the mountain slope seemed to come closer. Carefully he inspected each yellow rock, each deep black shadow and fissure. But only the shadows moved as the sun sailed steadily on.

But then, as Suron shifted his gaze to the upper slopes, he saw a shadow which moved in the opposite direction and then disappeared behind one of the large fangs of rock which a recent earth tremor had split from the main body of the mountain.

There was, after all, a living creature out there. A man?

Suron was sure that no man could survive in the heat unless he had protective clothing.

A visitor, then, from one of the inner worlds?

Impossible. No spaceship could survive the immense gravitational forces which now existed in space. And there was no matter receiver still operating on Tanet-tur-Taac.

Suron wondered if the creature had come from a near-by galaxy.

He reached a decision. Still staring at the slope, he waited patiently for the evening.

It was now never completely dark on Tanet, but when the sun had reached the farther horizon and the moon had begun to heave its monstrous bulk over the tops of the mountains and the sky turned to deep blue and the stars once again made their appearance, Suron left Rion-va-mëy, city-machine of Inevitable Hope.

On his naked back he wore a light force-field pack which would protect him against the elements and propel him over the rocks.

Drifting a few inches above the ground, he flew against the wind as clouds thickened and obscured the sky, bringing the first snow of the evening.

Suron increased his body temperature to counter the cold and when the snow flakes fell on his naked shoulders they melted immediately.

Behind him the city had changed colour. It was now a peculiar shade of orange. Suron knew that its resources were almost exhausted. The sea covered more of the towers and those towers which remained had begun to sway and to shake again.

Suron reached the foothills of the mountains and began to ascend.

The sky turned to a rich purple and the wind slashed the clouds so that the moon could be seen again. It was even closer. Suron almost felt he could reach up and touch it. It dominated the landscape.

Peering ahead he thought he saw the moving shadow, near the summit of the mountain. He increased his speed.

He reached the summit. The wind was so strong now that he was forced to use more power in order to stop himself being hurled from his position. The moon seemed to threaten to crush him, seemed to fill the entire sky.

An anthropoid quadruped emerged from behind a rock just below him. It was clinging to the slope, its hairy body rimed with snow, its fur flattened by the wind. It looked at him from its intelligent eyes and Suron recognized it.

He gasped.

The anthropoid moved its head and stared at him warily. It opened its mouth and spoke but the wind's yell swamped the words.

Suron moved down the slope towards the creature.

The alien retreated and disappeared. Suron saw that the rock hid a fissure in the slope – a cave.

Without hesitating, Suron entered the cave.

Light came. The cave was artificial. It was a room – possibly one of a series of rooms – and its contents had largely been smashed or thrown about by the tremors. On its four legs the creature stalked across the room, skirting the litter, and seated itself upon an oddly shaped chair. Gravely it regarded Suron.

'I thought your species extinct,' Suron said. Then he

frowned. 'Do you understand my tongue?'

The reply was clear, firm, musical. 'I understand it. My species was – extinguished. It was destroyed by your species a long time ago.'

'I did not know that,' said Suron.

'There was vegetation and beauty. There was peace. Ages ago your folk came with fire and burned all the beauty away, killed all my race save me. I hid, far underground. Then your folk went away. I could never discover why they destroyed our world.'

'How came you to learn our language?'

'A traveller.' The creature gestured with one of its hands and Suron saw a skull. It was the skull of a pre-hermaphroditic man. It must have been centuries old.

'You killed him?'

'He died. We were friends, I think.'

'Did he not know why your planet was burned.'

'He spoke of a war. He said this world had probably been a potential tactical position – something of that sort. He said that if they had known of us they might not have burned the planet but they assumed that creatures which walk on four legs are not 'intelligent' – whatever that had to do with it.'

'My ancestors once made distinctions between beings who reasoned like them and beings of a less questioning disposition.'

'Those who were content were destroyed.'

'It has been put thus. But you survived all these years.'

'Yes – in order to die, it seems, with those who robbed me of my happiness. Is this catastrophe another of your actions?'

'I do not think so. I am called Suron-riel-J'ryec.'

'I am Mollei Coyshkaery. Then what has caused this?'

Suron explained.

The anthropoidal creature seemed amused. 'So none win. What happened to us now happens to you.'

'With one difference. There will be none to remember mankind when it is gone.'

'It is all it deserved.'

The cavern shuddered.

'I suppose it is.'

'You are not like my friend.' Mollei indicated the skull. 'You are calmer – you look different.'

'Our race had begun to evolve into an altogether dissimilar species. As you are, we were almost immortal. We had no conflict among ourselves, no enemies to threaten us. We spent our time in adapting to what you see before you. We would have changed further, but . . .' Suron paused. 'And we had learned the habit of love,' he said. 'We had forgotten the habit of hate.'

'I have not yet learned to hate,' said Mollei. 'And now it is too late.'

'I am sorry.'

'You think it good to hate?'

'I think it good to know all feelings.' Suron's gaze was drawn back to the skull.

Mollei brushed melted snow from his fur. His expression was contemplative. 'There used to be music,' he said. 'I have heard no music for so long.'

'Perhaps you will hear it again?'

'What do you mean?'

'Some think that the galaxy undergoes a perpetual cycle of birth, death and rebirth – that its history is repeated over and over again with only minor differences.'

'But that means I will know the pain again. Your words bring no comfort, Suron-riel-J'ryec.'

Suron sighed. 'I admit that the conception is also terrifying.'

'You seem unmoved by what is about to happen.'

'It is inevitable, Mollei Coyshkaery.'

The cavern tilted. In spite of his force field Suron was hurled to the far wall. Objects slithered with him. The skull struck the wall and shattered. Mollei tried to save himself but was flung down and lay just below Suron, shouting in pain, trying to rise. Rock fell from the ceiling. There was a mighty roaring everywhere as the cavern continued to shake. Then it was still.

Suron lowered himself to the angle of floor and wall where Mollei lay. There was misery in the alien's eyes. Some of his bones were evidently broken.

'That was the worst,' Mollei murmured. 'What caused it, I wonder . . .'

'The moon has fallen at last. Some distance from us, I would think.'

'What does that mean?'

'It means that in a short while your planet will be drawn into its sun almost at the same moment that the sun joins other stars. We are all moving towards the centre, Mollei. A few hours after we are dead there will be a single mass comprising what was once our galaxy. After that, it is believed, the mass will explode and the galaxy will begin again.'

'Death comes quickly,' gasped the alien, 'but life takes such a long time to form ...'

'Will you come with me to Rion-va-mëy, my city?' Suron asked. 'There is the means, there, to ease your pain.'

'I am dying,' said Mollei. 'Let me die alone.'

'Very well.'

Suron sought the entrance to the cave, but it had been blocked when the moon had fallen. He went back to the dying alien. 'I am trapped, it appears.'

Mollei raised himself on his elbow and pointed to a doorway. 'There are several other exits. One of them may still not be blocked.'

'Thank you.'

'Good-bye, Suron-riel-J'ryec.'

'Good-bye.'

Suron knew that the power was beginning to fail in his pack. He drifted through the dark doorway and widened his eyes so that he could see into the murk of the next room. There were pictures here and artefacts of all kinds. He realized that Mollei had used the cave system as a museum – a monument to his slain race. Suron experienced what he thought might be guilt.

He made his way through several similar chambers, pausing only to stare at a very ancient relief which seemed to indicate that Mollei's people had once had indigenous enemies – it was a scene of warfare. The ape creatures were triumphantly driving away some kind of similarly armed epicene people.

And then he saw a rent in the roof and light was coming through.

Suron increased the power and moved up to the ceiling, passing through the crack and out on to the surface of the planet.

He gasped as the light struck his eyes and he covered them with his hands. He knew that there was little power left in his pack but he increased the strength of the field still further and shut out the burning heat and the light as much as he could.

He looked down the mountain and away to the sea.

The sea was boiling. Clouds of steam swirled around what was left of Rion-va-mëy. Huge black fissures split the mountain. As fast as he dared, he began to descend.

The screen around his body faltered. Suron knew he would